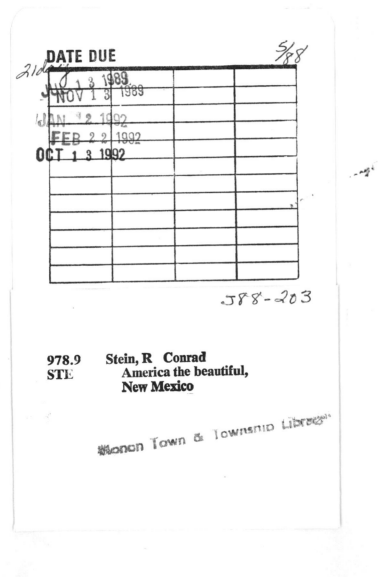

978.9   Stein, R Conrad
STE   America the beautiful,
         New Mexico

AMERICA the BEAUTIFUL
NEW MEXICO

By R. Conrad Stein

Consultants

J. Paul Taylor, former Associate Superintendent for Instruction, Las Cruces Public Schools

Jean Craven, District Coordinator for Social Studies, Albuquerque Public Schools

Don E. Alberts, Ph.D., Chief Historian for Kirtland Air Force Base; President, Historical Research Consultants, Albuquerque

Genevieve Jackson, Principal, Nizhoni Elementary School

Robert L. Hillerich, Ph.D., Bowling Green State University, Bowling Green, Ohio

CHILDRENS PRESS®

CHICAGO

The Rio Grande near Taos

Project Editor: Joan Downing
Assistant Editor: Shari Joffe
Design Director: Margrit Fiddle
Typesetting: Graphic Connections, Inc.
Engraving: Liberty Photoengraving

Childrens Press®, Chicago

978.9
S

Library of Congress Cataloging-in-Publication Data

Stein, R. Conrad.
    America the beautiful. New Mexico / by R. Conrad Stein.
        p.   cm. — (America the Beautiful state books)
    Includes index.
    Summary: Introduces the geography, history,
government, economy, industry, culture, historic sites, and
famous people of the Land of Enchantment.
    ISBN 0-516-00477-8
    1. New Mexico—Juvenile literature. [1. New
Mexico.] I. Title. II. Series.
F796.3.S74   1988
978.9—dc19   87-34113

Civic Plaza in Albuquerque

TABLE OF CONTENTS

Chapter 1

THE UNIQUE STATE

THE UNIQUE STATE

New Mexico is like no other American state. Its people are a distinctive mixture of Native Americans, Hispanics, blacks, and Anglo Americans. Its history includes an ancient golden era, a 250-year period of Spanish rule, a raw Wild West epoch, and the birth of a nuclear age. Its countryside possesses haunting beauty.

How different is New Mexico? A surprising number of Americans seem to believe it is a foreign land rather than an American state. A family that moved from Florida to New Mexico was informed by its credit card company, "We do not mail credit cards outside of the continental United States." A Nebraska man who announced his intention to retire in New Mexico was told by a co-worker, "You should do well down there because you get a lot of pesos for the dollar."

But this image of New Mexico as a foreign land is undeserved. Not only is New Mexico very much American, it is one of the most interesting states in the country. There is a certain magic in the air of New Mexico—an unexplainable force that has inspired native New Mexican artists for centuries and drawn generations of artists and writers to the state. The magic is felt in the state's lively cities, along its lonely mountain peaks, and among the ruins of its amazing ancient civilizations. Anyone who has ever lived in New Mexico and experienced its excitement knows that the state genuinely warrants its nickname—the Land of Enchantment.

Chapter 2
THE ENCHANTED LAND

THE ENCHANTED LAND

[New Mexico is] a perfectly mad looking country—hills
and cliffs and washes too crazy to imagine all thrown up
in the air by God and let tumble where they would.
—New Mexican artist Georgia O'Keeffe

GEOGRAPHY AND TOPOGRAPHY

New Mexico is a southwestern state. Spreading over 121,666
square miles (315,127 km), it is the fifth-largest of the fifty states.
Only Alaska, Texas, California, and Montana surpass it in size.
The state is rectangular in shape except for a small "boot heel" at
its southwestern corner.

On the east, New Mexico shares a border with Oklahoma and
Texas. On the south, it borders Texas and Mexico. Arizona lies to
the west, and to the north is Colorado. The boundary lines of the
state's northwest corner intersect with the borders of Arizona,
Utah, and Colorado to form the only place in the nation where
four states meet. This region is often referred to as the Four
Corners area.

Topographically, New Mexico can be divided into four sections.
The eastern third of the state is an extension of the American
Great Plains. Here, much of the land is as flat as that in Nebraska.
In the state's north-central section, the southern Rocky Mountains
rise suddenly and dramatically. Southwestern and south-central

Whereas northeastern New Mexico is covered by vast plains (left), the northwestern part of the state is a region of desert valleys and dramatic rock formations such as Enchanted Mesa (above).

New Mexico are part of the Basin and Range Region, where mountains alternate with areas of flat desert land. Northwestern New Mexico, part of the Colorado Plateau, has valleys and plains punctuated by cliffs, canyons, and steep rock formations.

The Continental Divide, which marks the geographic division between rivers flowing toward the Atlantic Ocean and those flowing toward the Pacific, zig-zags through the plateaus in the western third of the state.

A LAND OF INFINITE VARIETY

New Mexico has provided the backdrop for many motion picture Westerns. In a typical Western, John Wayne is shown leading a troop of horsemen over a dusty plain studded with chimney-shaped, flat-topped rocks. These tall pillars of the sky are often nestled between tablelands called mesas—the Spanish word for table. Some of these steep-sided mesas are broad and harbor woodlands on their flat tops, while others are quite narrow.

Mesas and fantastic rock formations are among the state's most popular tourist attractions. Shiprock, in the northwestern part of the state, resembles a lonely ship in full sail. Cleopatra's Needle is a delicate rock that looks like a sewing-piece used by a sky goddess. Carlsbad Caverns, a dizzying maze of limestone caves, is world famous.

New Mexico stuns visitors with an endless variety of landscapes. The mountaintops are cloaked with thick forests. Streams filled with fish tumble through the mountains, and deer and other wild animals are plentiful. Yet, a short distance from forests bristling with life are deserts so barren that even cactus plants must struggle to survive.

About one-fourth of New Mexico is forested. Lush woodlands are found in the highlands and in the mountain valleys. The state has seven national forests, the largest of which is the Gila National Forest in the southwest part of the state. The commonly found piñon, or nut pine, is the New Mexico state tree. During winter months, New Mexicans cheer up their living rooms by burning piñon in the fireplace. The unforgettable pungent fragrance of piñon smoke is a signature of New Mexico.

Yucca, the New Mexico state flower, is found throughout the state. Yucca plants have stiff, pointed leaves that Indians once

New Mexico's incredibly varied landscape ranges from the Sangre de Christo Mountains (top left, bottom right), to White Sands National Monument (top right), to Frijoles Canyon (left), to the Bisti Badlands (bottom left).

Horses grazing in the Rocky Mountain region near Abiquiu

used to make rope, baskets, and sandals. First-time visitors to New Mexico are amused by the antics of tumbleweed. Tumbleweed is the popular name for several bushy, beach-ball-shaped plants that break away from their stems and, driven by the wind, spread seeds by bouncing over the ground. Tumbleweed is a menace during the dry months because it can easily spread forest and brush fires.

In 1950, a small bear cub was found trembling on a tree branch after a fire destroyed his home in New Mexico's Lincoln National Forest. His rescuers named him Smokey, and a national symbol was born. In the 1950s and 1960s, Smokey the Bear was the mascot for the national drive to prevent forest fires. In 1963, in Smokey's honor, the New Mexican legislature chose the black bear to be the official state animal.

The Rio Grande (left), which runs the length of
New Mexico, has been dammed off in the south-central
part of the state (above) to create Elephant Butte
Reservoir, the state's largest lake.

RIVERS AND LAKES

Although New Mexico overflows with natural beauty, nature
was stingy in providing the land with water. Lakes and rivers
make up only .002 percent of the state's total surface area—the
lowest water-to-land ratio of all fifty states. Redistribution of
water to aid farming, industry, and home development has long
been a hotly debated political issue.

The state's largest and historically most important river is the
Rio Grande, which snakes through the central mountain country
and eventually flows southeast to form the border between Texas
and Mexico. The second-largest river, the Pecos, winds southward
through the eastern section of the state. The Canadian River
drains northeastern New Mexico. Most of New Mexico's lakes are
man-made reservoirs that serve as part of a complicated water
conservation and distribution program. Elephant Butte Reservoir,

A lightning storm on the northeastern plains

the state's largest, was formed by a dam on the Rio Grande. Other man-made lakes are Navajo Reservoir on the San Juan River, Conchas Lake on the Canadian River, and Lake McMillan on the Pecos River.

CLIMATE

Visitors to New Mexico are sometimes surprised to see residents hanging clothes on a line during the middle of a light rainstorm. There is nothing foolish about this practice. Residents know that a New Mexico shower rarely lasts long, and that the sun will soon return to make the clothes crispy dry.

New Mexico's northern mountains average 20 inches (50.8 centimeters) of total precipitation (rain and snow) a year. The state's many deserts receive less than 10 inches (25 centimeters) a year. By contrast, the state of New Jersey averages 46 inches (117 centimeters) of total precipitation a year. Nevertheless, New Mexico is subject to sudden storms so violent that the ground cannot absorb the sheets of rain. So, strangely,

The northern mountain region (left), which includes forests of ponderosa pine (above), receives the heaviest snowfall in the state.

bone-dry New Mexico is sometimes the victim of a flash flood.

Snow can fall anywhere in the state, but in the mountains it often piles up almost to treetop level. A healthy layer of snow in the mountains is vital because the spring melt feeds the state's parched streams and rivers. Summers in the mountains and the high plateaus consist of warm days and pleasant nights. The summer season is intolerably hot in the southeast, where the land dips below 3,000 feet (914 meters) above sea level. The highest and lowest temperatures ever recorded in the state were 116 degrees Fahrenheit (47 degrees Celsius) at Artesia in June 1918 and Orogrande in July 1934, and minus 50 degrees Fahrenheit (minus 45 degrees Celsius) at Gavilan in February 1951.

In winter or in summer, New Mexico remains the Land of Enchantment. As writer Oliver La Farge put it, "Those who live with [New Mexico] before their eyes learn to follow the constantly shifting moods, the delicate and incessant changes of light from day to day and from hour to hour, which give that empty-seeming country a life of its own."

Chapter 3
THE PEOPLE

THE PEOPLE

POPULATION

The 1980 census listed 1,303,445 people living in New Mexico, an increase of almost 30 percent over the 1970 figure. In the late 1980s, it was estimated that the population had topped 1.5 million. This recent population surge makes New Mexico one of the country's fastest-growing states.

Although it is expanding rapidly, New Mexico ranks only thirty-seventh among the states in population. Its population density is 11 people per square mile (4 people per square kilometer), making it one of the most thinly populated of all the states. North Carolina, for example, has a population density of 124.6 people per square mile (49 people per square kilometer).

The vast majority of residents make their homes in the Rio Grande Valley, which runs through the center of the state. Almost 70 percent of New Mexicans live in cities and towns. In order of population, New Mexico's five largest cities are Albuquerque, Santa Fe, Las Cruces, Roswell, and Farmington. Santa Fe is the state capital.

THE TRICULTURAL SOCIETY

New Mexicans love to celebrate. They call their parties *fiestas*, the Spanish word for festival. The Fiesta de Santa Fe, held in mid-September, celebrates the return of Spanish colonists to Santa Fe

The people of San Ildefonso Pueblo perform a Buffalo Dance on their annual feast day, January 23.

in the 1690s after they had been driven out by the Pueblo people in 1680. In summer, the various Pueblo Indian groups celebrate the planting and harvesting of crops by dancing and feasting in their villages. In the town of Lincoln, a "Billy the Kid" pageant held in August honors the frontier era when Americans from the East pushed into the New Mexican wilderness. These various events illuminate New Mexico's tricultural society.

Men and women from many ethnic groups live and work in New Mexico, but three groups—"Anglo" Americans, Hispanic Americans, and American Indians (also called Native Americans)—dominate the state. Those known as Anglo Americans, or simply Anglos, make up the majority. Men and women of Hispanic descent make up 33 percent of the population, and Native Americans comprise 7 percent. About 2 percent of the population is black, and 1 percent is of Asian origin.

Most Americans consider an "Anglo" to be a white Protestant whose ancestors came from northern Europe. But in New Mexico, the term is used in a more general way to describe the non-Spanish white people who live in the state. Many of the state's Anglos are descendants of hardy pioneers who carved out homes in New Mexico after the Civil War. The Anglos are the wealthiest of the three groups, and they often wield a great deal of political power.

Old families from New England like to boast that their ancestors were the first to bring European civilization to what is now the United States. But that claim is false. A European colony was established in New Mexico by Spaniards in 1598—nine years before the founding of Jamestown, and twenty-two years before the Pilgrims arrived at Plymouth Rock. Many of the original Spanish colonists intermarried with the Indians. Today, the descendants of the early Spaniards are referred to in New Mexico as Spanish Americans, Hispanics, or Hispanos.

In recent years, fresh waves of immigrants from Mexico and other Latin American countries have come to New Mexico. These immigrants, combined with the Spanish Americans who have lived in the state for generations, give New Mexico the highest percentage of Hispanic men and women in all fifty states.

New Mexico is an exciting mix of Hispanic (left), Anglo (right),
and Native American cultures.

Native American and Hispanic art, architecture, and culture
have molded New Mexico. The distinctive, flat-roofed houses
made of adobe (sun-dried brick) that one finds throughout the
state were developed by the Pueblo Indians. Murals—magnificent
wall paintings that are the pride of Mexico—adorn many public
buildings. Street fairs boast Spanish music and folk dances.
Numerous Hispanic leaders have risen to positions of power in
the state.

When the Spaniards first came to the American Southwest, they
found that some Indians lived in established towns, while others
were nomads with no permanent homes. The Spaniards called the
village-dwellers *Pueblos* after the Spanish word for towns. The
Pueblos were not a single tribe, but several groups of people who
shared a common culture, but not necessarily a common
language. To this day, New Mexican Indians are divided into the
Pueblo and the once-nomadic tribes, even though this too-simple
division does not properly define the very complex cultures of
Native American peoples.

The Pueblo people of the Southwest have lived in the same

Above: A Navajo sheep rancher tending his flock
Right: A young participant in a foot race held
during the fall festival at the Jicarilla Apache
Reservation

location longer than any other culture in the nation. Nineteen
Pueblo groups now live in New Mexico. Their towns (also called
pueblos) look much as they did centuries ago. New Mexico's
nineteen pueblos are Acoma, Cochiti, Isleta, Jemez, Laguna,
Nambe, Pojoaque, Sandia, San Felipe, San Ildefonso, San Juan, San
Lorenzo, Santa Ana, Santa Clara, Santo Domingo, Taos, Tesuque,
Zia, and Zuñi.

The so-called nomadic groups of New Mexico are the Jicarilla
Apaches, the Mescalero Apaches, the Utes, and the Navajos. For
the most part, these peoples have given up their nomadic
existence. Although they live throughout the state, the majority
reside on reservations.

The Mescalero Apache Reservation, in the southeastern part of
the state, is a beautiful land of lush valleys and forested
mountains. The Mescaleros own and operate an elegant resort and
ski lodge. On their reservation in north-central New Mexico, the
Jicarilla Apaches raise horses and cattle, and operate several

lucrative mines. Some Utes live along New Mexico's northern border, but the majority reside in Utah and Colorado.

The Navajos are the nation's largest Native American group, with a population of about 160,000. Once the nomads of unbounded land, the Navajos now occupy a reservation that covers 14 million acres (5.7 million hectares) and spills into Arizona and Utah. The Navajos operate coal mines, oil fields, lumber mills, electric generating stations, and agricultural enterprises. They are also master craftsmen, and make and sell beautiful silver items and rugs.

RELIGION

In the weeks before Christmas, the streets of many New Mexico towns are lined with paper bags aglow with tiny candles. These candles, or luminarias, light the way for a group of children who carry statues of Joseph and Mary as they knock on doors asking for shelter. They are trailed by a priest and a church congregation. When the travelers are finally invited inside a house, the crowd pours in to greet the host family with hugs and laughter. This colorful ceremony, called *Las Posadas*, has its origins in Mexico. It is one example of how Spanish culture has influenced the Catholic church in New Mexico.

Most New Mexicans are Christian. Catholics form the largest Christian group. All major Protestant denominations are represented in the state. Mormons have lived in New Mexico for more than a century. Jewish synagogues stand in the major cities.

Indians may follow Christianity, their traditional beliefs, or a blending of the two. A large number of Indians see no reason why their ancient beliefs should be totally replaced by a Christian god and the Christian religion. So they attend Christian services, but

Luminarias (also called farolitos), which decorate many New Mexico towns at Christmastime, recall the old Spanish custom of making small bonfires to light the way to the church on Christmas Eve.

may also take part in traditional dances or ceremonies. Other New Mexican Indians reject Christianity entirely and continue to worship solely as their ancestors did. Traditional religious practices vary from group to group. Generally, those who follow traditional religions believe in a single creator and a host of lesser spirits. They also recognize the existence of a spirit world, which, though elusive, can be visited for brief periods.

LANGUAGES

In 1986, Californians made English the official language of their state. A year later, the New Mexican legislature turned down a similar proposal after just two hours of debate. "We are proud of our cultural diversity," said Representative Albert Shirley, himself a Navajo. "I hope we can tell the rest of the United States that we like to be different in New Mexico." The state's constitution, in fact, officially states that New Mexico is a bilingual state.

One out of three families in New Mexico speaks Spanish in the home. In some isolated villages, "old-line" Hispanics speak a form of Spanish similar to that used in Spain four hundred years ago. Sometimes, new immigrants from Mexico or Latin American countries are surprised when they hear this archaic dialect.

English is the common tongue in New Mexico. Most Hispanics speak both Spanish and English. Anglos who have grown up in the state know at least a few words of Spanish, and some are fluent in the language. Many New Mexican Indians speak their traditional tongue, Spanish, English, and maybe a few words of another Indian language.

New Mexico scholar Marc Simmons tells the story of a young doctor who began his practice working in an Albuquerque hospital. Because of a high fever, one of his elderly patients was unable to remember anything but his traditional language. The doctor asked an Indian nurse to translate.

"Sorry. I can't help you," said the nurse. "That man is a Navajo and I am a Pueblo." A puzzled look overcame the doctor. "But you both speak 'Indian,' don't you?" he asked.

A Navajo or an Apache speaking his or her tribal language may not be able to communicate with a Pueblo. An Ute speaking a Shoshone dialect will fail to be understood by the Apaches, the Navajos, and most of the Pueblos. In fact, among the nineteen Pueblo groups, four distinct languages are spoken.

New Mexico's tricultural society can be confusing to outsiders, but residents view it as a gift from the past—when three peoples met, fought, and finally learned to live in peace. Today, the three cultures live as a family, and like all things New Mexican, their family history is different and exciting.

Chapter 4
THE BEGINNING

THE BEGINNING

The Creator made the world—come and see it.
—A prayer said by the Pima people of
the American Southwest

BEFORE HISTORY

Thousands of years ago, people migrated from Asia to the Americas. These people were the distant ancestors of the men and women Christopher Columbus mistakenly called Indians. The American Southwest was one of the first regions where these ancient people gathered and began a settled life. In the Sandia Mountains near Albuquerque, archaeologists have uncovered a cave dwelling holding human artifacts that are at least twenty thousand years old. Numerous archaeologists suggest that the American Southwest is the most ancient human-settled site in the Western Hemisphere.

The first New Mexicans were hunters who killed animals with spears and clubs. Their prey included mammoths, mastodons, giant sloths, American camels, and other exotic beasts that became extinct thousands of years ago. As early as 4000 B.C., these people began planting crops, finding farming an easier and far more dependable source of food than stalking and killing animals. In Bat Cave along New Mexico's western plains, ears of corn that date from 3000-2000 B.C. have been found.

The Gila Cliff Dwellings in southwestern New Mexico were inhabited by a branch of the Mogollon people from about A.D. 1 to 1300.

New Mexico's first true farmers were the Mogollon people, who appeared in the southern part of the state near the Arizona border about two thousand years ago. In addition to farming, the Mogollon people built villages, worshipped at large communal lodges, and fashioned excellent clay pottery. For generations, they were the cultural leaders of the Southwest, until their dominance was replaced by another dynamic people.

THE RISE OF THE ANASAZI

The Spaniards who pushed into New Mexico in the 1500s were astounded by the great adobe-and-stone cities they found. Even though many were in ruins, they stood as silent testimony to a once-marvelous civilization. When the Spaniards asked the Native Americans who had built the fabulous cities, the Native Americans answered in a tone of deep respect, "The Anasazi," meaning "the Ancient Ones."

The Anasazi were the ancestors of the people now called Pueblos. Anasazi civilization began with a people known as the

Basketmakers, whose culture emerged around A.D. 1 and lasted about seven hundred years. The Basketmakers were highly skilled at weaving baskets from weeds, grasses, and human hair. The baskets were so tightly woven that they held water with almost no leakage. Archaeologists searching in caves have found examples of their baskets that, because of New Mexico's dry climate, are remarkably well preserved.

Around A.D. 500, the Basketmakers began living in villages, some of which contained as many as a hundred houses. The houses had dug-out floors, short brick walls, and roofs. These simple huts were the forerunners of the grand Anasazi buildings that so amazed the Spaniards.

THE GOLDEN AGE OF THE ANASAZI

From about 700 to 1100, descendants of the Basketmakers made great progress in the arts, architectural engineering, and the agricultural sciences. This development stage ushered in what scholars call the Great or Classical Period of the Anasazi Culture, which lasted from 1100 to 1300. It was an epoch when cities rose, trade increased, and the arts and sciences flourished. It was truly the golden age of the Anasazi civilization.

Anasazi buildings are the most striking legacy of the Classical Period. Construction was most prevalent in what is now the Four Corners area, where the borders of New Mexico, Arizona, Colorado, and Utah meet. More than twenty-five thousand Anasazi sites have been identified in New Mexico alone, and at least that many are known to exist in Arizona.

The most spectacular Anasazi cities stood in Aztec and Chaco canyons in northwestern New Mexico. They featured multi-storied cliff dwellings, made of sandstone bricks, that could be

Pueblo Bonito, which once rose five stories and had more than eight hundred rooms, is the most impressive surviving example of the fine sandstone-masonry buildings constructed by the Anasazi people.

compared to modern apartment buildings. One building, Pueblo Bonito, had eight hundred rooms and could house more than a thousand people. Nowhere else within the borders of the United States did people of that time build such impressive structures.

The Anasazi also built hundreds of miles of arrow-straight roads to neighboring cities or to centers of worship. A typical road was thirty feet (nine meters) wide and graded to be both smooth and hard. At the time, it was the finest network of roads constructed anywhere north of Mexico. But why did the ancient Pueblo people build these magnificent roadways? They had no animal-drawn vehicles and traveled only on foot. Scholars guess that the roads had religious significance.

A spectacular example of Anasazi engineering is a great sundial built on a mesa near Chaco Canyon. Discovered in 1977, the sundial consists of huge stone slabs that allow daggerlike slices of sunlight to strike a target of circular lines. By reading the position of sunlight along the lines, an Anasazi priest could predict the seasons precisely and be able to tell farmers the best times to plant and harvest.

New Mexico's dry climate has preserved such remnants of Anasazi culture as rock carvings, or petroglyphs (top left); pottery, pottery shards, and ears of corn (above); and the ruins of such dwellings as Pueblo del Arroyo at Chaco Culture National Historical Park (left).

During the Classical Period, the Anasazi cultivated the fields that surrounded their cities. They watered the dry, unyielding land through an intricate irrigation system. Corn, the staple crop, was kept in storage bins for use during the winter and in times of drought. In addition to corn, the Anasazi grew beans, squash, and melons, and raised turkeys to eat on special feast days. They also hunted deer and antelope with a throwing device called an *atlatl* that enabled a hunter to hurl a spear with deadly force.

The art of pottery making flourished during the Classical Period. Archaeologists have uncovered beautiful Anasazi vases covered with intricate geometric designs or marvelous pictures of birds. The people wove fine cotton cloth adorned with bright pictures. Their jewelry was magnificent. Some Anasazi necklaces contain a thousand or more precisely worked stones. The Anasazi also were students of medicine and knew and used the healing power of at least seventy different medicinal plants.

These ancient Pueblo people were not a nation, a single tribe, or even a language group. In fact, on rare occasions, rivalries between Anasazi cities exploded into warfare. Each city practiced self-government, drawing its laws from ancient religious commandments. Some scholars maintain that Anasazi life declined when the cities outgrew their old form of government.

Religion dominated the life of the ancient Pueblo people. Their buildings centered around a dance court and ceremonial chambers called kivas. The Anasazi believed that no harm would come to their society as long as they maintained a spiritual brotherhood among themselves, the forces of nature, and the gods.

THE TIME OF CHANGE

History shows that most golden ages are shortlived. The Anasazi's finest hour ended when the people began abandoning their cities in the late 1200s and early 1300s. Since the Anasazi had no written language, today's scholars have few clues as to what led to the great change.

Drought and warfare are the two factors that most likely forced the Anasazi to forsake their old and cherished way of life. By examining the rings of trees growing at the time, archaeologists have been able to determine that a murderous dry period scorched

The Great Kiva at Aztec Ruins has been restored to look as it did when it was used as a ceremonial chamber by the Anasazi.

the Southwest for twenty-three years during the late 1200s. At the height of this rainless spell, small bands of nomadic, often aggressive, hunter-gatherers—the ancestors of the Navajos and the Apaches—drifted onto and raided the Anasazi cities for food.

The ancient Pueblos were never a unified people, and when they abandoned their cities, they marched their separate ways. The Hopis relocated in northeastern Arizona, the Tanos and the Keres settled along the Upper Rio Grande in north-central New Mexico, and the Zuñis established towns near what is now New Mexico's western border. Pueblo people remain at these sites today. The migration was orderly, and the people brought their culture with them.

The great migration caused subtle changes in the ancient Pueblo lifestyle. Their rock paintings shifted from religious scenes to scenes of angry warriors and the trials of battle. Perhaps the people had fallen into the trap of fighting among themselves, or perhaps raids from the nomadic groups had become more deadly. But during this troubled time, the religious beliefs of the Pueblos remained as unshaken as the earth itself. As their conquerors soon discovered, these were people who preferred death to spiritual surrender.

Chapter 5

THE SWORD AND THE CROSS

THE SWORD AND THE CROSS

"I take possession, once, twice, and thrice, and all the times I can and must, of the . . . kingdom and province of New Mexico." With these words, spoken in 1598, Don Juan de Oñate established the first Spanish colony in the province of New Mexico.

THE CURIOUS VISITOR

From out of the hills near the Zuñi pueblo of Hawikúh came a small band of Indians whose dress indicated that they were not a Pueblo people. It was April of 1539. Leading the group was a black man. The Zuñi leaders stared. Never had they seen such a person. What manner of man was he?

He was Estevanico, a North African slave and the lead scout of a Spanish exploring party headed by a priest named Marcos de Niza. Estevanico had much experience dealing with the Indians of the Southwest. For eight incredible years, he and three Spaniards had wandered across the country after they were shipwrecked on the Texas coast. During that time, Estevanico befriended many of the Indians he met. Some thought he and the Spaniards had magical powers, and urged them to heal their sick.

At Hawikúh, however, Estevanico's good fortune with the Indians ended. The Zuñis took up bows and arrows and killed him and several of his Indian companions. Historians still debate about the reasons for the slayings. Perhaps, increasing warfare between the Pueblos and the nomadic peoples made the Zuñis wary of all strangers. Perhaps Estevanico arrogantly demanded gifts. Or perhaps the Zuñis were insulted by Estevanico's outrageous story that behind him were men whose skin was the color of snow, and who rode on the backs of four-legged animals larger than deer.

GOD, GOLD, AND GLORY

About 2,000 miles (3,218 kilometers) south of the land of the Pueblos, Spaniards were settling into the newly conquered territory of Mexico. The Spaniards, fierce soldiers with horses and superior weapons, had defeated the mighty Aztecs in 1521. In the New World, the Spanish invaders were in search of gold, military conquest, and converts to Christianity. Their mission in the Americas could be summed up in three words: God, gold, and glory.

Rumors filtered back to the Spaniards that vast riches lay in the little-known country north of Mexico. False stories persisted that somewhere in the northern deserts rose the fabulous Seven Cities of Cíbola—treasure towns where even the poor ate on plates of solid gold.

To find these fantastic cities, the Spaniards marched north with a force of eleven hundred soldiers and Mexican allies. Commanding the party was a dashing young nobleman, Francisco Vásquez de Coronado. His men were so confident of finding riches similar to those they had discovered in Mexico that they called the land to the north *un nuevo Mexico*—a new Mexico. Hence the entire region, and later, the American state, received its name.

Sixteenth-century Spanish *conquistadores*, who marched northward into New Mexico in search of new land, gold, and converts to Christianity, sometimes fought with Pueblo Indians who refused to bow to their rule.

Coronado's expedition lasted from 1540 to 1542. His men explored parts of present-day Arizona, New Mexico, Texas, Oklahoma, and southern Kansas. In his frustrating search for the seven golden cities, Coronado marched from valley to valley, and from pueblo to pueblo. But he found neither cities of wealth nor gold. Disappointed, he returned to Mexico City.

Among the Pueblo Indians, Coronado and his men had left a trail of terror. The Pueblos had for the most part greeted the Spanish travelers courteously, but rebelled when Coronado demanded that they worship a new god and swear allegiance to the king of Spain. In battle, the Indians were at the mercy of weapons they had never seen before—iron swords and shields, booming muskets, and horses that allowed the soldiers to travel and fight at will.

In 1581, a priest named Augustín Rodríguez and army captain Francisco Sánchez Chamuscado visited New Mexico. In 1582, explorer and merchant Antonio de Espejo wrote a glowing report about the fertile lands he saw along New Mexico's riverbanks. The report intrigued Spanish officials, for they viewed land as second in value only to bright metals.

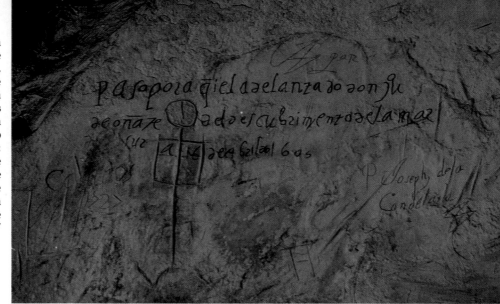

On his way back from an expedition to the Gulf of California, Don Juan de Oñate carved a message in Spanish into what is now known as Inscription Rock. Translated into English, it reads: "Passed by here the Governor Don Juan de Oñate from the discovery of the Sea of the South on the 16th of April, 1605."

SPANISH SETTLEMENT

A strange procession rolled along the Rio Grande Valley in the spring of 1598. The column, which extended almost four miles (six kilometers), was made up of a unit of Spanish soldiers, their wives and children, scores of oxen pulling wagons, and thousands of cattle, sheep, and pigs. Unlike the adventurers of the past, these Spaniards intended to colonize the land of the Pueblos.

Leading the march was a wealthy businessman, Don Juan de Oñate. Oñate claimed "all the provinces and kingdoms of New Mexico" for Spain and became the colony's first governor. At the confluence of the Rio Grande and the Chama River, his party set to work building two villages, which they called San Juan and San Gabriel. Thus began Spanish colonization of the New Mexico region.

Following their custom of ruling by the sword and the cross, Spanish leaders demanded that all nearby Indians honor the king of Spain and convert to Christianity. The Acomas, the most independent of the Pueblos, resisted. Acoma, often called the "Sky City," was built on top of a towering mesa. To reach its walls, an

Acoma Pueblo, sometimes called the "Sky City" (above), was attacked by the Spaniards in 1599.

invader had to scale a cliff of sheer rock. After a fierce battle, the Spaniards managed to secure one of Acoma's two entrances. Once inside, Spanish soldiers slaughtered eight hundred Acoma defenders. Indians who surrendered were tortured and enslaved.

The massacre at Acoma infuriated other Pueblo groups and led to sporadic warfare between the Indians and the Spaniards. To add to their troubles, the settlers' supplies began to run dangerously low. Dozens of Spanish soldiers began deserting the colony because they still believed the century-old legend that somewhere in the Southwest were seven cities of pure gold. In 1610, Governor Oñate was replaced by Pedro de Peralta, who ordered the colonists to abandon San Gabriel. He led them south to an uninhabited spot near the upper Rio Grande, where he founded a new capital—Santa Fe.

The Palace of the Governors in Santa Fe is the oldest government building in the United States.

Santa Fe was built around a central square used mainly by the military and called the Plaza de Armas. The town's first large building was the Palace of the Governors, which housed the office of the governor and other high-ranking military leaders. Houses and churches spread out from the plaza. From the churches, priests ventured into the New Mexican wilderness to bring the word of Christ to the Indians.

During periods of peace, the Spanish settlers and the Pueblos exchanged ideas and goods. The Spaniards planted new food crops such as barley, wheat, oats, onions, peas, watermelons, peaches, and apples. They also introduced sheep, cattle, and horses—three animals that revolutionized the economy of the Southwest. The Indians reciprocated by giving the Spaniards piñon nuts and the special corn that grew in their region.

THE PUEBLO REVOLT

By the late 1600s, Spanish settlement was almost a hundred years old, but only about twenty-five hundred Spaniards lived in

Among the many Spanish missions built in New Mexico in the 1600s were Nuestra Señora de los Angeles, the ruins of which can still be seen at Pecos National Monument (above); and San Miguel de Socorro in Socorro (inset).

New Mexico. Most of these colonists were concentrated along the upper Rio Grande. Santa Fe was the only sizable Spanish town. Clusters of Spanish-owned ranches extended from Taos to the tiny village of Isleta. Such places as Jemez and Pecos were simply Indian pueblos that had been given Spanish names by the Europeans. Mission churches stood at Acoma and even at the remote Zuñi pueblos.

The issue of religion caused a great deal of conflict in New Mexico. Spanish priests believed tribal dancing and other Indian rituals were a form of witchcraft and were therefore condemned by the Bible. The priests persuaded army leaders to punish those Pueblos who insisted on practicing their traditional beliefs. Indians who refused to denounce their faith and accept Christianity were jailed, whipped, and even hung.

Sporadic revolts against the Spaniards broke out in the pueblos of Jemez, Isleta, Alameda, San Felipe, and Cochiti. Occasionally,

Pueblo groups attempted to drive the Spaniards out of New Mexico by allying with their ancient enemies, the Navajos and the Apaches. Each rebellion was brutally put down by Spanish soldiers.

At San Juan Pueblo, a man named Popé was one of hundreds who suffered imprisonment and public whipping rather than denounce his religious beliefs. A superb organizer, Popé brought together Pueblo leaders and drew plans for a joint military attack against the Spaniards. Never before had the diverse Pueblo groups cooperated so closely.

On August 10, 1680, Indians swarmed out of Taos, Pecos, Santa Cruz, and several other pueblos. They burned churches, killed priests, and then marched toward Santa Fe. Soon the cornfields outside the Spanish capital seethed with warriors.

A horrible battle erupted that lasted nine days. One out of five colonists was killed. Those able to walk fled across a scorching desert trail that was referred to as *Jornada del Muerto* (Journey of the Dead). The survivors gathered at the mission of El Paso del Norte (present-day Juarez, Mexico).

In Santa Fe, the Pueblo warriors celebrated their glorious victory. Soon, however, tribal leaders began quarreling with each other. Never a unified people, the Pueblo groups went their separate ways once their common enemy had been defeated. When Popé died in 1692, the last vestige of a Pueblo coalition passed away with him.

In 1692, a dozen years after the Pueblo Revolt, a Spanish army unit approached the ruins of Santa Fe. Its commander, an officer named Diego de Vargas, implored the Indians to surrender the city, promising that no harm would come to their leaders. Years of fighting had demoralized the Pueblos, and after a heated debate, they threw down their arms and allowed the Spaniards to enter

The annual Fiesta de Santa Fe celebrates the return of Spanish colonists to New Mexico in the 1690s.

the city. Santa Fe was recaptured without bloodshed. Within a few years, the rest of New Mexico had been reclaimed by the Spanish as well.

Once their power had been reinstated, the Spanish priests resumed their efforts to convert the Pueblos to Christianity. This time, however, understanding that the Pueblos' traditional beliefs were deeply ingrained, the priests were more willing to allow the Indian and Christian religions to exist side by side. The religion of the Pueblos has survived many conquerors, and today it is viewed by them as a light that will shine until eternity.

LIFE IN SPANISH NEW MEXICO

In theory, New Mexico was ruled by authorities in Mexico City, who, in turn, took their orders from Spain. However, instructions from Mexico City took many weeks to reach Santa Fe, and Spain was half a world away from the American Southwest. Because of its isolation, New Mexico governed itself without day-to-day direction or intervention from outside authorities.

The province of Spanish New Mexico included all of present-day New Mexico, most of Colorado and Arizona, and slices of

Utah, Wyoming, Kansas, Oklahoma, and Texas. Although Spain laid claim to all of this enormous region, it actually controlled only the Rio Grande Valley near Santa Fe.

During the 1700s, two distinct social classes emerged in the province: the *pobres* (poor ones) and the *ricos* (rich ones). Most of the ricos were of pure Spanish blood, while the pobres were of mixed Spanish and Indian ancestry. In Mexico, where the mixing of the two populations first began, people of such ancestry were called *mestizos*. Today, most New Mexican Hispanics are mestizos. A small middle class of merchants, artisans, and owners of small sheep and cattle ranches also began to grow at this time.

The ricos were merchants and landowners. Most of them owned large tracts of land that had been granted to them or their forbears by the Spanish king. They were hardworking people who took seriously the management of their huge ranches. The men were immensely proud of their horsemanship. The women were trained in music and the household arts. Weddings, baptisms, and other festive religious events were lavishly celebrated by these people of wealth.

The pobres owned small farms, tended the cattle and sheep of the ricos, or produced and sold food items, handcrafts, or religious images commissioned by the church. The pobres were devout Catholics. In remote areas, the Catholic faith was kept alive by those who were part of a spiritual brotherhood called the *Penitentes*. The Penitentes sought forgiveness for their sins through physical pain. During Easter Week, some of them carried heavy crosses while allowing others to whip their backs until blood flowed. A few Penitentes were even actually crucified. This extremely devout group functioned as a kind of social-service agency for their villages. They took care of the sick and the poor, recited prayers for the dead, and conducted other religious services.

Although the Spanish settlers lived in relative peace with the Pueblos, they were unable to pacify the nomadic groups. Horses, which the Spaniards had introduced to the southwestern Indians, greatly increased the fighting capability of the nomadic warriors. The Apaches quickly became superior horsemen. The northern settlements, where the pobres lived, were favorite targets for raiding Apaches. Over the years, the Spanish governors waged war against the Indians, but achieved no lasting success.

Even though they lived in a harsh and sometimes dangerous land, the Spanish settlers found ways to enjoy themselves. Religious celebrations ranged from a solemn procession on Easter Sunday to the fireworks of a saint's feast day. Even prisoners were free to celebrate on feast days, because jailers abandoned their posts to attend dances. One traveler wrote about a New Mexico town, "to judge from the quality of tuned instruments that salute the ear almost every night of the week, one would suppose that a perpetual carnival prevailed everywhere."

Spanish law forbade the settlers from trading goods with any nation other than Mexico. Foreigners were not even allowed in New Mexico without special permission. Because of these rigid laws and the desolate lands that surrounded their colony, New Mexicans in the eighteenth century often remained unaware of international events occurring beyond the borders of New Mexico. As New Mexico historian Ruth Armstrong has written, "The American Revolution might just as well have been on another planet for all the difference it made to the Spaniards of New Mexico."

A new era began, however, when American president Thomas Jefferson purchased the huge Louisiana Territory from France in 1803. Suddenly, New Mexico had a young but ambitious neighbor whose sights were set on expansion to the Pacific shore.

Chapter 6

THE AMERICAN CENTURY

THE AMERICAN CENTURY

> In the vicinity of Santa Fe, land is very good and can be had at low prices. The climate is healthful and the seasons mild and delightful.

> The fiendish Apache roams at will over the vast, arid plains and among the lonely gorges of a large portion of the territory [of New Mexico], ever on the watch for blood and booty.

These are two contrasting views of New Mexico, both written by American settlers in the mid-1800s.

THE AMERICANS ARRIVE

After a difficult trek over mountains and deserts, a Louisianian named Baptiste Lalande arrived in Santa Fe in 1804. With him were a string of packhorses bearing goods owned by an Illinois merchant. Lalande liked what he saw. He sold the goods, and rather than taking the profits to his boss in faraway Illinois, pocketed the money and decided to stay.

A remarkable parade of Americans journeyed to New Mexico early in the nineteenth century. One was army officer Zebulon Pike, who, in 1806, explored the little-known lands west of the Mississippi River. After sighting the magnificent mountain now known as Pike's Peak, he and his men blundered into New Mexican territory and were arrested by the Spanish army. Pike

Above: Zebulon Pike
Right: The Santa Fe Trail
in the mid-1800s

later published a book that painted a shining picture of New
Mexico and fired the dreams of American frontiersmen.

THE MEXICAN PERIOD

In the fall of 1821, church bells pealed and cannons fired
booming salutes in Santa Fe and neighboring villages. Word had
reached the capital that the eleven-year-long Mexican
independence movement had finally succeeded. Having won its
freedom from Spain, Mexico was now a sovereign state. The New
Mexican governor called the bells and cannon bursts "the sweet
voice of liberty."

New Mexico was now a province of Mexico. Once in power, the
Mexican government took the bold step of allowing New
Mexicans to trade with their American neighbors. A Missouri
merchant named William Becknell immediately took advantage of
the new policy. In 1821, he and a party of men entered Santa Fe
and sold American-made products to a horde of eager buyers. The
next year, he returned in a wagon train with more men and more
products. The two trips brought him a fortune in profits.

Becknell's success brought a stampede of merchants to Mexico
via a route that became known as the Santa Fe Trail. This 800-mile

(1,287-kilometer) pathway wound from Independence, Missouri to Santa Fe. The trail crossed harsh terrain where hostile Indians or bandits often waited in ambush. Only the bold and adventurous made the trip. The Santa Fe Trail became the most storied route in the American push westward.

During the glory days of the Santa Fe Trail, the sleepy New Mexican capital burst into excitement whenever American wagon trains approached. Village boys usually spotted the caravan first and raced each other into town shouting, *"¡Los Americanos! ¡Vienen los Americanos!"* ("The Americans! Here come the Americans!") Everyone dropped what they were doing and crowded into the Plaza to eye the new goods brought by the Yankees.

During this period, a colorful breed of American fur trappers pushed into New Mexico. Known as the mountain men, they were restless, free spirits who always longed to glimpse the unseen land beyond the next mountain. In winter, the mountain men gathered at Taos, which they turned into the fur-trading center of the Southwest. They also gave the town a collection of racy saloons and gambling halls.

The Mexican period lasted for twenty-five years. Then, in the 1840s, a political tide rose in the east—a tide that Mexico was unable to stem.

NEW MEXICO BECOMES AMERICAN

In a magazine published during the 1840s, an American writer declared it was "our manifest destiny to overspread the continent." The word *manifest* means obvious or evident, and *destiny* is a predetermined course of events. Together, the two words represented the idea that the territorial expansion of the United States was a movement that *must* happen, as if God had ordained it. Manifest destiny became an American crusade. Extending America's boundaries to the Pacific Ocean, however, required seizing the Mexican territories of New Mexico and California.

The first "invasion" of New Mexico came in 1841 from citizens of the newly formed, independent Republic of Texas. General Hugh McLeod of Texas led a trading unit of three hundred horsemen across the border, hoping that their presence would cause the New Mexican people to throw off the yoke of Mexico and join Texas. But the Texans were captured and brought before New Mexican governor Manuel Armijo, who executed some and sent the rest to Mexico City for trial.

In 1846, war broke out between the United States and Mexico. The two immediate causes were a boundary dispute and the admission of Texas into the Union. But certainly the excitement generated by the manifest destiny crusade helped spur American leaders into the conflict.

An American army led by General Stephen W. Kearny stormed into New Mexico in August of 1846. Unlike the rag-tag invaders from Texas, this army was a well-equipped cavalry unit of seventeen hundred men. New Mexican troops were overmatched, and Kearny took Santa Fe without firing a shot.

A new flag—the Stars and Stripes—fluttered over Santa Fe's central square. New Mexicans gathered in the Plaza, stunned and confused, sensing that their old, Spanish-based way of life was lost. The highest-ranking Mexican official, Juan Vigil, told the saddened crowd, "To us the power of the Mexican Republic is dead. No matter what her condition, she was our mother. What child does not shed abundant tears at the tomb of his parents?"

But not all New Mexicans accepted defeat passively. A last stand against American authority began at Taos and gathered strength as it spread along the Rio Grande. An army of fifteen hundred New Mexican men assembled at the town of La Cañada. In January of 1847, they were defeated by American troops.

The 1848 Treaty of Guadalupe Hidalgo ended the Mexican War. Mexico was forced to cede California and New Mexico to the United States. Five years later, the Gadsden Purchase gave New Mexico its present southern border. Originally, New Mexico Territory included all of Arizona and parts of Colorado, Nevada, and Utah. The boundaries of present-day New Mexico were drawn by Congress in 1863. Settlers from the eastern and southern states began migrating to New Mexico in the early 1850s.

New Mexico Territory became embroiled in the American Civil War when a Confederate force entered the region from Texas. The Confederates won the bloody Battle of Valverde, fought near the city of Socorro, and marched on to occupy Albuquerque and Santa Fe. New Mexico loyalties were divided during the war. Recently arrived settlers, most of whom were from the South, favored the Confederates. The majority, however, merchants and old-line Hispanic residents, were pro-Union. The final Civil War battle in

New Mexico was at Glorieta Pass near Santa Fe. During that fight, Manuel Chavez, a Hispanic officer, demonstrated his loyalty to the Union by leading volunteers from Colorado to the wagon train where the Confederates kept their supplies. The destruction of those supplies allowed Union forces to drive the southerners out of New Mexico, and upset Confederate plans to extend their power west to California.

THE INDIAN WARS

In 1862, the Union army sent General James Carleton to New Mexico to subdue the Navajos and the Apaches. For the next four years, Carleton ruled the territory as if he were a military dictator. "There is to be no council held with the Indians, nor any talks," was his written order. "The men are to be slain whenever and wherever they can be found. The women and children may be taken prisoners, but, of course, they are not to be killed."

Carleton needed a wily officer who knew not only the Southwest, but also the habits of the Indians. He called on a man who became a folk hero: Christopher "Kit" Carson.

Kit Carson first traveled the Santa Fe Trail as a youngster in 1826. He later became a mountain man, working the fur trade in the Rockies and wintering in Taos. Like many mountain men, he felt more comfortable in the presence of Indians than he did surrounded by the trappings of white society. Fluent in Spanish, Carson later settled in Taos, where he married into a prominent Hispanic family. He understood the problems of New Mexico's Hispanics and Indians and was trusted by both. He disagreed with Carleton's harsh policies, but as a military officer felt it his duty to obey his general's orders.

In southern New Mexico, leading the newly formed 1st New

The Kit Carson House in Taos (left) was the residence of the famous frontiersman (right) from 1843 to 1868.

Mexico Volunteer Cavalry, Colonel Kit Carson pounced on the Mescalero Apaches. Within three months, he had defeated the Indians. A few hundred were gathered together and forced to move to Bosque Redondo, a reservation on the Pecos River. Then, Carleton and Carson turned their attention to the Navajos.

Unlike the Apaches, the Navajos had learned small-scale farming, sheep herding, and weaving from the Pueblos and from the Spanish. Also, many of their elders wanted to make peace with the powerful Americans. But General Carleton insisted that the Navajos leave their ancient territory, walk across the width of New Mexico Territory, and resettle on the inhospitable Bosque Redondo reservation. From there, they would no longer be able to raid the Rio Grande settlements. When the Navajos refused to leave, war began.

Kit Carson waged a scorched earth campaign, burning Navajo cornfields and peach trees and slaughtering flocks of sheep. A note in his log said that in one day his men laid ruin to "large quantities of pumpkins and beans and not less than one hundred acres of as fine corn as I have ever seen." Two million pounds (.9 million kilograms) of grain were wiped out in less than a year, causing starvation among the Navajos.

In 1864, the Navajo people were forced to leave their homeland and resettle on reservation land at Bosque Redondo (right) near Fort Sumner.

The Navajos were too scattered and did not possess the rifles and cannons needed to challenge Carson's swift cavalry. The end came in 1864, when Carson invaded the Navajo stronghold at Canyon de Chelly and met only feeble resistance. However, instead of killing all the men and boys, as Carleton had ordered, Carson spared the lives of all who surrendered.

In the midst of a dreadful winter, eight thousand Navajos were forced on a terrible 300-mile (483-kilometer) trek through snowy, windswept mountains to the reservation at Bosque Redondo. The Indians had little food, and some were barely clothed. Hundreds died on the trail. Sympathetic to their plight, Kit Carson wrote frantic letters to army authorities pleading for food and blankets for the marchers. His letters were ignored. Today, the Navajos refer to this tragic journey as the "Long Walk."

Resettlement efforts at Bosque Redondo were a total disaster. The marginal soil was unable to produce enough crops to feed the thousands of Indians gathered there. More than two thousand people died of starvation and disease. In 1868, the federal government conceded failure and allowed the Navajos to return to their traditional homeland in the Four Corners region. Ever since that time, the Navajos have called the awful years at Bosque Redondo the *Nahondzod*—the "Fearing Time."

THE LAWLESS YEARS

WANTED: BILLY THE KID
I will pay $500 reward to any person or persons
who will capture William Bonney, alias The Kid,
and deliver him to any sheriff in New Mexico.
Lew Wallace, Governor

Billy the Kid was a baby-faced young man who wore what
seemed to be a peaceful smile. He was also a chronic outlaw and
a ruthless killer. "The Kid" was just one of many desperadoes
who roamed New Mexico during the years that followed the
Civil War. A brief look at his career illustrates the lawlessness of
the era.

William Bonney, whose real name was Henry McCarty, was
probably born in New York City. When he was thirteen, he came
to Silver City, New Mexico with his mother. His first brush with
the law came two years later, when he was jailed for a minor
offense. He escaped by worming his way up the jailhouse
chimney. When he was seventeen, a blacksmith made the
mistake of insulting him. Billy the Kid shot the man in his
tracks. Before he was gunned down by a sheriff, the Kid claimed
to have killed twenty-one men—"one for every year of my life."
He robbed, rustled cattle, and constantly evaded the law. For a
few months in 1878, he worked as a gunman for a powerful
rancher who was battling merchants in a bloody feud known as
the Lincoln County War.

At least eight novels have been published romanticizing the
Kid's criminal career. One such book was written by Pat Garrett,
the sheriff of Lincoln County and the man who finally shot and
killed Billy the Kid. Garrett claimed, "Those who knew him best
will tell you that in his most savage and dangerous moods his

Legendary outlaw Billy the Kid (far right), who was gunned down by Lincoln County sheriff Pat Garrett in 1881 (above), is buried in the town of Fort Sumner (right).

face always wore a smile. He ate and laughed, drank and laughed, rode and laughed, talked and laughed, fought and laughed—and killed and laughed.''

New Mexican sheriffs worked for pitifully low pay while trying to bring law and order to a territory where guns were bought and sold in saloons. One of the most revered sheriffs was Elfego Baca of Socorro County. A Hispanic, he spoke both Spanish and English and was respected by the Hispanos as well as by the Anglos. His bravery under fire was the stuff of legends. In 1882, from a cabin near the village of Frisco, Baca held off a band of cowboys for thirty-six hours. When the smoke cleared, even the

This 1880 photograph shows a locomotive pulling out of the station at Glorieta, New Mexico, a stop on the Atchison, Topeka, and Santa Fe line.

broomstick hanging from the cabin wall was riddled with bullets. After retiring as sheriff, Baca entered a more peaceful profession. He practiced law in Albuquerque until his death in 1945.

Adding to the dangerous mood of the times were Apache warriors who rampaged through the entire Southwest. They fought under a succession of chiefs—Cochise, Victorio, Nana, and finally, Geronimo. Most of their raids took place in Arizona and south of the New Mexican border in Mexico, but the fighting often spilled over into New Mexico Territory. Even famous Indian fighter General George Crook failed to subdue the fierce Apache braves.

CHANGE AND PROGRESS

New Mexico's first railroad line was laid in 1878. Three years later, the Atchison, Topeka, and Santa Fe Railroad connected the cities of Raton, Las Vegas, Albuquerque, Socorro, and Deming,

Mining towns such as Chloride sprang up in New Mexico in the late 1800s and early 1900s.

while the Southern Pacific line became the first transcontinental line to cross southern New Mexico. The railroads changed the lives of isolated New Mexicans more than any other single industry. Train service also stimulated the growth of the mining and cattle businesses.

Railroads brought in prospectors and sophisticated equipment needed for modern mining operations. At Lake Valley, miners discovered silver in veins so pure that the metal could be sawed off in blocks instead of having to be dug out by traditional

A New Mexico cattle ranch in the 1890s

methods. Mining towns such as Chloride, Hillsboro, and White Oaks sprang up like weeds. Many of these towns were abandoned, however, as soon as the minerals ran out.

Cattle ranching in the territory expanded as Texans moved into its southeastern region. Soon this area became known as "Little Texas." Some New Mexican cattle ranches spread over 30 to 40 square miles (78 to 104 square kilometers) of land. One of the richest of the early New Mexican cattle barons was John Chisum. From his headquarters near Roswell, Chisum directed about a hundred cowboys herding sixty thousand head of cattle.

At the end of the century, some politicians in the East questioned whether New Mexico, with its large Hispanic and Indian populations, would be loyal to the United States if the country went to war. The answer came when the Spanish-American War broke out in 1898. Half the members of Theodore Roosevelt's Rough Rider Regiment were volunteers from New Mexico, and a Hispanic, Maximiliano Luna, was one of the officers who led the famous charge up Cuba's San Juan Hill.

Chapter 7
THE
ATOMIC AGE

THE ATOMIC AGE

Despite the economic progress New Mexico made in the late 1800s, most Americans living at the turn of the century viewed it as a dusty, backward, frontier territory. The *Chicago Tribune* declared, "New Mexico has but a few oases amid its volcanic deserts." This widespread but mistaken attitude persisted until late in the twentieth century, when New Mexico finally became recognized as a leader in the arts and sciences.

STATEHOOD

Congress had created the Territory of New Mexico in 1850. For sixty-two years, the region remained a territory, its citizens denied the full rights and privileges enjoyed by other Americans. Bigotry, both racial and religious, was one factor that kept New Mexico out of the Union. In 1876, when the idea of granting New Mexico statehood was being debated, the *Milwaukee Sentinel* unfairly remarked, "The scum and dregs of the American, Spanish, Mexican, and Indian people are there concentrated." Mining companies, railroads, and cattle ranches operating in New Mexico opposed statehood because they feared it would mean higher taxes.

Those opposing statehood were finally overruled on January 6, 1912, when, after an act of Congress, President Taft officially

63

In 1912, the Taos Society of Artists was formed by a group of artists that included Ernest Blumenschein, Bert Greer Phillips, Joseph Sharp, and Irving Couse.

proclaimed New Mexico the forty-seventh American state. At a White House ceremony, the president said to New Mexican delegates, "I am glad to give you life. I hope you will be healthy." The news touched off a fiesta more joyous than anything New Mexicans had seen in years. Cannons and fireworks boomed, and brass bands blared patriotic tunes. According to one newspaper reporter, a huge crowd gathered at the Plaza in Santa Fe and "cheered themselves hoarse over the victory."

THE GROWING YEARS

At the turn of the century, artists from the East and the Midwest began drifting into New Mexico. They gathered at Taos, and in 1912 formed the Taos Society of Artists. Soon, novelists, poets, and still more artists flocked to New Mexico. These talented and

President Woodrow Wilson sent American troops into Mexico to pursue Mexican revolutionary Pancho Villa (left) after he and his men raided the border town of Columbus, New Mexico in 1916.

educated men and women created some of the liveliest art colonies in the country.

To the south, a civil war raged in Mexico. One of that war's leading figures was a revolutionary named Francisco "Pancho" Villa. In March 1916, about a thousand of Villa's men raided the border town of Columbus, New Mexico. They set houses on fire and murdered sixteen citizens. Enraged, President Woodrow Wilson sent General John Pershing and a troop of six thousand cavalrymen into Mexico with orders to bring back Villa, dead or alive. Despite Pershing's considerable efforts, however, the crafty Villa escaped capture.

In 1930, a Massachusetts scientist named Robert Goddard came to New Mexico to test rocket-ship models. Goddard was a visionary who believed that someday huge rockets would send men and women into space. In other places, Goddard had been denounced as a crackpot. New Mexicans however, had long tolerated artists, poets, and mad scientists. In fact, New Mexican cowboys enjoyed chasing after Goddard's spent rockets. No one at that time could have guessed that the aerospace industry would someday become one of New Mexico's leading industries.

During the 1930s, the entire country was gripped by the Great Depression. In New Mexico, mines closed, and railroads and cattle ranches laid off workers. A cardboard and scrap-lumber shantytown built by the homeless rose on the southern fringe of Albuquerque, which had grown to be the state's largest city.

THE NUCLEAR AGE

Swiftly and without fanfare, a group of strangers bought a little-used boys' school located on a lonely ranch west of Santa Fe. Few people even knew that the ranch site was called Los Alamos. It was 1943, and the fears and frustrations of World War II gripped the state. New Mexico sent seventeen thousand men overseas, and early in the war had the highest casualty rate of any state in the Union. Soon, dozens of newcomers were seen arriving in Santa Fe, hurrying to cars, and being whisked off to the ranch at Los Alamos. Local people simply shook their heads at the mysterious goings-on. No one suspected that a secret laboratory was being created at Los Alamos, and that scientists there were working on the Manhattan Project, a plan to build the most dangerous weapon in all of human history.

On July 16, 1945, in the desert near Alamogordo, New Mexico,

New Mexico was first used as a scientific testing ground in 1930,
when scientist Robert Goddard (left) arrived to experiment with rockets.
Fifteen years later, the desert of south-central New Mexico became the
testing ground for the world's first atomic bomb (right).

the first atomic bomb was tested. It burst into a dazzling ball of
pure orange light. Temperatures inside the ball were greater than
that of the sun. The desert sand beneath the blast site melted and
fused into glass. Scientist Robert Oppenheimer, a key creator of
the bomb, watched the horrific explosion from a bunker. To his
fellow scientists, he whispered a line from the ancient Hindu book
the *Bhagavad-Gita*: "Behold, I have become death, destroyer of
worlds."

World War II ended shortly after atomic bombs obliterated the
Japanese cities of Hiroshima and Nagasaki. For better or for
worse, the nuclear age had dawned in New Mexico.

POSTWAR DEVELOPMENTS

After World War II, the federal government poured money into New Mexico, changing the state's economy forever. The once-secret city of Los Alamos became a huge nuclear laboratory housing hundreds of scientists and their families. Nuclear research spilled into Albuquerque with the construction of sprawling Sandia National Laboratories. To test the latest rockets, the government created the White Sands Missile Range on the same land where the first atomic bomb had been exploded.

To staff the many new laboratories, highly educated scientists and engineers moved to the state. New Mexico soon had the highest percentage of people with Ph.D.s (doctoral degrees) of any of the states. Albuquerque doubled in size between 1950 and 1960. The popular magazine *The Saturday Evening Post* claimed, "New houses go up [in Albuquerque] in batches of fifty to three hundred at a time, and transform the barren mesas before you get back from lunch."

But New Mexicans paid a price for prosperity based on weapons production. A storage depot for atomic bombs was built on a mountain near Sandia Laboratories. Many people wondered what would happen if there were an accidental explosion.

A potentially horrific accident occurred on May 22, 1957, when a hydrogen bomb broke loose from a bomber and fell on open land near Albuquerque. The bomb did not explode and was removed from the ground by Air Force crews. Not until 1981 did this near-calamity become known to the general public.

To test bombs and missiles, the government and the military needed enormous tracts of land. In 1953, hoping to expand its missile range, the army tried to purchase a ranch owned by a feisty eighty-two-year-old named John Prather. Mr. Prather had

Los Alamos National Laboratory, established in 1943, is the nation's most important weapons development center.

worked the land for fifty years, and told the army his ranch was not for sale at any price. A judge ordered Prather to vacate the land, but the old rancher refused to budge. Finally, army officials tried to scare Prather by warning him that powerful missiles might buzz his ranch house. Prather became a folk hero admired by the entire nation when he replied, "I'm not afraid of missiles. I've raised mules all my life."

MODERN NEW MEXICO

In the 1960s, New Mexico was forced to confront an issue that had been left unsettled for more than a century—land ownership. At the conclusion of the Mexican War, the United States had promised to honor all land-ownership claims held by Hispanic residents in the Southwest. For the most part, Hispanics kept their individually owned farms and ranches when the Americans took possession of New Mexico. But Spanish law had given large tracts of land to entire villages, and the American government did not recognize community-owned land. Over the years, the land that was once village-owned was bought up or simply taken over by ranchers, most of whom were Anglos.

In the mid-1960s, many years after the Hispanics of the northern county of Rio Arriba had lost their community land, a Mexican-American preacher named Reies Tijerina arrived from Texas. He claimed that New Mexicans of Spanish descent had been cheated out of thirty-five million acres (fourteen million hectares) by Anglos and the American government. The people of impoverished Rio Arriba, where one of every two people was on welfare, listened to Tijerina's passionate speeches. "For us, the land is the mother," he said. As the leader of a militant organization called the Alianza Federal de Mercedes, Tijerina led marches and attempted to seize federal lands in order to force the government to reopen land-claim cases. In June 1967, he and armed members of the Alianza took over the Rio Arriba County Courthouse. Hostages were taken, and two officers were shot and wounded. Governor David Cargo had to call out the National Guard to restore order.

In 1970, a different land dispute was settled when a congressional act granted the people of Taos Pueblo permanent possession of beautiful Blue Lake. The lake, which had been public land for many years, was considered sacred by the Taos people. Although the Blue Lake issue was settled peacefully, the question of land ownership remains a smoldering issue in the state.

The 1980s began on a note of horror as inmates at the overcrowded New Mexico Penitentiary rioted. The disorder began on February 2, 1980, when inmates took several guards hostage. For thirty-six hours, the prisoners fought among themselves, settling old scores with homemade knives and clubs. When order was finally restored, thirty-three inmates were dead, twice that number were injured, and $14 million-worth of property was damaged.

When Democrat Toney Anaya was elected governor in 1982, he

Thirty-three prisoners were killed and millions of dollars' worth of property was damaged when inmates of New Mexico Penitentiary rioted for thirty-six hours in February 1980.

promised to crack down on rising crime in the state. However, he told voters that his religious convictions would forbid him to commit a person to death while he served. True to his word, no prisoner was executed during Anaya's term, even though pro-death-penalty politicians were popular in neighboring states. In one of his last acts as governor, Anaya commuted the sentences of five convicted murderers from death to life imprisonment.

Republican Garrey Carruthers, who succeeded Anaya as governor, took over a mixed economy. The state's nuclear and high-tech industries flourished. In 1987, New Mexican firms were awarded $1.8 billion in contracts to build the highly controversial SDI or "Star Wars" missile defense system. But despite a booming nuclear industry, much of rural New Mexico remained poor, and pockets of poverty existed in many towns.

On the same desert grounds where today's space-age missiles are tested, ten-thousand-year-old arrowheads have been found. New Mexican history has ranged from arrows to atoms, has embraced Indian, Spanish, and Anglo cultures, and has touched millions of lives. Few states can claim such a distinctive past.

GOVERNMENT AND THE ECONOMY

GOVERNMENT AND THE ECONOMY

In New Mexico, one out of four people works directly for the federal government. Hundreds of civilians are employed at such military facilities as Kirtland Air Force Base near Albuquerque and White Sands Missile Range near Las Cruces. The state and local governments are also major employers. To continue its growth and progress, New Mexico requires contributions from both the government and private businesses.

GOVERNMENT

New Mexico's state constitution was adopted in 1911. The constitution provides for three main branches of government: the executive branch, which carries out laws; the legislative branch, which creates laws; and the judicial branch, which interprets laws. In theory, each branch acts as a check on the power of the others.

The governor is the chief officer of the executive branch. He is elected to a four-year term, and may serve two terms in a row. The governor's powers include having the authority to call out the state militia in times of emergency, appointing key people to state jobs, and approving or vetoing (rejecting) proposed laws sent to him by the legislative branch. Other powerful members of the executive branch are the lieutenant governor, the attorney general, the secretary of state, the auditor, and the treasurer.

The kiva-style
State Capitol
in Santa Fe

The legislative branch is made up of a forty-two-member senate
and a seventy-member house of representatives. Senators serve
four-year terms; members of the house serve two-year terms. The
legislature debates proposed laws (called bills) and sends the final
copy of a bill to the governor. When a bill is signed by the
governor, it becomes state law.

The judicial branch is headed by a supreme court that has five
members. The supreme court can strike down laws that it decides
violate the state constitution. The court system also tries people
accused of committing crimes. The state has a court of appeals
with seven justices. The state's principal trial courts are the
district courts, presided over by fifty-seven district-court judges.

New Mexico has thirty-three counties. County government is
especially important in the rural areas, where the county
courthouse is not only a seat of political power, but also a place to
meet old friends and socialize.

To a certain degree, New Mexico's Indian reservations function
as states within a state. In these enclaves, tribal law may supersede
state law. For example, many pueblos have an office of village
governor, a legacy from the time when the Pueblos were ruled by
powerful chiefs.

The University of New Mexico at Albuquerque is the state's largest university.

EDUCATION

Maintaining the public-school system is the state government's largest expense. In recent years, it has cost about $3,000 a year to educate each student. The state's average classroom size is nineteen pupils per teacher. State law requires that all children between the ages of five and sixteen attend classes.

Public education was almost nonexistent in New Mexico until the end of the nineteenth century. During the Spanish era, the only real schools in New Mexico were those set up by priests to train other priests or to convert Indians to Christianity. This changed somewhat in the 1850s, when Bishop Jean Baptiste Lamy, a man with unbounded energy and determination, set up several schools in the Santa Fe area. Yet, as late as 1888, there was not a single public college or high school in the entire territory. Those who wanted an education had to depend on private or parochial schools. After the establishment of a public school system in 1891, the state made great gains in education.

Today, New Mexico has six major state universities and several branch colleges, community colleges, and vocational schools. The publicly financed University of New Mexico at Albuquerque is the state's largest university. It has a sprawling campus and is noted for its excellent engineering and anthropology departments. Other fine state schools are New Mexico State University in Las Cruces; and New Mexico Institute of Mining and Technology in Socorro, a

Two important aspects of New Mexico's economy are scientific research, such as the nuclear energy research carried out at Sandia National Laboratories (left); and the mining of such minerals as oil (right), natural gas, uranium, potash, copper, and coal.

small school with excellent engineering and mining programs. Important private colleges are St. John's College in Santa Fe, located in a gorgeous setting on a windswept hill outside the capital; and the College of Santa Fe.

MINING AND NATURAL RESOURCES

Vast riches lie beneath New Mexico's soil. Oil and natural gas were discovered in the 1920s, and since that time have become a major industry. In 1950, a Navajo sheep herder named Paddy Martinez found uranium ore in the northwest part of the state. Today, New Mexico leads the states in producing this mineral.

Annual mining revenues total $6 billion. The state is a major producer of coal, zinc, copper, gold, silver, and perlite. Most mines are found in the western third of the state. New Mexico is the

Left: Handwoven Navajo rugs displayed in Taos
Right: Indian jewelry for sale at the Santa Fe Plaza

country's leading source of potash, an important component of commercial fertilizer.

MANUFACTURING AND TECHNOLOGY

New Mexico's most productive factories turn out weapons and other products for the aerospace industry. The state is at the forefront of scientific research, with facilities devoted to developing aerospace, electronics, and medical technology, as well as military and non-military uses of nuclear energy. New Mexico produces processed food, electrical machinery, plastics, lumber products, and glass products. Manufacturing employs 7 percent of the state's workers.

Handcrafts such as high-quality ceramics, woodcarvings, rugs, stone statues, and jewelry are a cottage industry with many Pueblo groups. The Navajos are noted for their fine rugs, blankets, and other weavings, as well as for their jewelry.

AGRICULTURE

Waiting for rain is a frustrating experience in New Mexico. Traditional dry farming (farming accomplished without

Above: Cowboys roping cattle on a ranch in El Rito
Right: An irrigation canal in Portales

irrigation) is carried out mainly on the eastern plains, where wheat, corn, cotton, and sorghum grain are grown. New Mexico's soil will produce lush crops when irrigated. In irrigated fields along the Rio Grande, farmers raise fruit, nuts, chile peppers, and vegetables. About 55 percent of New Mexico's cropland is irrigated.

New Mexico has far more sheep and cattle than people. Cattle raising, which was originally introduced by the Spaniards, is concentrated mainly in the eastern third of the state. Many sheep are raised in the central mountain region. The Navajos also raise thousands of sheep in the Four Corners region.

TRANSPORTATION AND COMMUNICATION

New Mexico has 15,000 miles (24,135 kilometers) of paved roads, and, surprisingly, more than 50,000 miles (80,450 kilometers) of dirt roads. People from outside the state are amazed by the huge network of unpaved roadways, which remain usable because of the dry climate. On the outskirts of Santa Fe, houses

New Mexico's climate is so dry that many roads, including this one in a residential area of Santa Fe, are left unpaved.

that cost half a million dollars or more may be served by unpaved roads.

Most of the state's 2,200 miles (3,540 kilometers) of railroad track are used to haul freight or bulk mineral ore. Passenger service between cities is scant. The famous Atchison, Topeka, and Santa Fe line still serves Albuquerque and other major cities.

New Mexico has about 140 airports, the busiest of which is Albuquerque International Airport. Only the Albuquerque airport can handle very large planes. Several other airports are served by regional airlines that use smaller aircraft; many serve only private, small aircraft. Farmington and Roswell have sizable passenger airfields. Santa Fe has no major airport, and residents have fought efforts to build one because they fear increased pollution and traffic congestion.

The state has twenty daily newspapers, ninety-five radio stations, and twelve television stations. The largest daily papers are the *Albuquerque Tribune* and the *Albuquerque Journal*. Many small-circulation literary magazines and newsletters announcing art shows and publishing new works are distributed among New Mexico's communities of artists and writers.

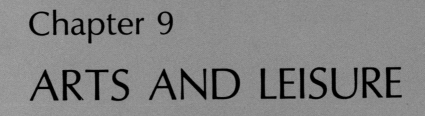

Chapter 9
ARTS AND LEISURE

ARTS AND LEISURE

THE FINE ARTS

No other state has an art tradition quite like New Mexico's. It began with Indian rock painters who left their masterpieces on the sides of cliffs. It included Spanish woodcutters who created exquisite icons for churches. Modern art in New Mexico flourished early in the twentieth century in the town of Taos.

Luck alone brought Joseph Henry Sharp to remote Taos in 1893. An artist and illustrator, Sharp became enraptured with the mountain scenery and the timeless way of life pursued by the region's Hispanics and Indians. He boasted about Taos to fellow artists Ernest Blumenschein, Bert Greer Phillips, and Irving Couse. Soon, an art colony was born.

The artists who moved to Taos in the early 1900s revered their Pueblo neighbors. Critics complained that they glamorized the Indians by painting idealized pictures of "noble savages." But Taos artists also studied Pueblo painters and sculptors to capture their spiritual approach to art. Said one critic, "To enjoy a Blumenschein, we must forget subject matter and revel in fantastic shapes and harmonious color. The Indian understands these attributes far better than our own people, who are often prone to order their art tempered with the ignorance that calls for photographic slavery to the details of nature."

Mabel Dodge, a wealthy New York art lover, visited Taos in 1916 and experienced a creative awakening. "My life broke in two

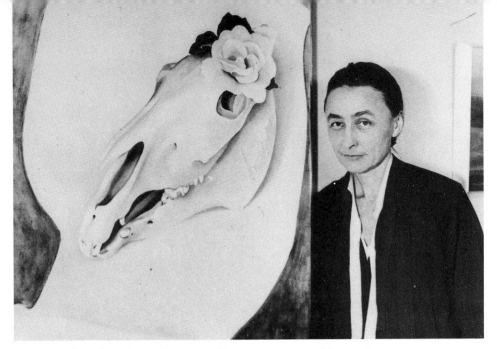

Georgia O'Keeffe, shown here standing next to one of her paintings, was inspired by the stark beauty of the New Mexico landscape.

right then," she said, "and I entered the second half, a new world that replaced all the ways I had known. . . ." After marrying a Pueblo Indian named Tony Luhan, she built an adobe-style mansion in Taos and threw it open to artists, writers, and assorted hangers-on.

While the Taos art colony grew, a group of Indian artists formed in Santa Fe. Known as the Self-Taught Painters, the group included Crescencio Martinez and his brother Julian. Noted Taos artist John Sloan wrote, "The Indian artist deserves to be classified as a Modernist. His art is old, yet alive and dynamic; but his modernism is an expression of a continuing vigor seeking new outlets, and, not like ours, a search for release from exhaustion."

One of America's most celebrated artists, Georgia O'Keeffe, fell in love with New Mexico during her first visit in 1929. Over a career that spanned more than sixty years, O'Keeffe painted New Mexico's gray hills and blazing sunsets countless times. She had a special fascination for animal bones, bleached white by the sun, lying half-buried in the desert sand.

San Ildefonso potter Maria Martinez (right), shown here with her husband Julian, was especially famous for her black-on-black pieces (above).

For more than two thousand years, the Pueblo people have created decorative pottery. Today, their work still thrives. Most modern Pueblo potters are women. Perhaps the most famous was Maria Martinez of San Ildefonso Pueblo. In the 1920s, Martinez sparked an artistic revival of Pueblo Indian art when she began earning recognition for her exquisite "black-on-black" pieces. Using an ancient potter's wheel, she continued to create beautifully designed bowls and vases until her death in 1980. Helen Cordero of Cochiti Pueblo is known for her charming "storyteller" figures. Margaret Tafoya of Santa Clara Pueblo often paints her pottery creations with pictures of bear paws. "They are good luck," she says. "The bear always knows where the water is."

In both pottery and jewelry making, each pueblo has its own distinctive style. Acoma potters produce delicate white pieces that are highly sought by collectors. Human and animal figures on Cochiti story-telling vases dramatize ancient legends. Zuñi

Clockwise from top left: A Navajo weaver; a Tesuque "Rain God"; artist R.C. Gorman; a Navajo sandpainting; Zuñi women wearing some of the intricate silverwork for which the Zuñi are famous

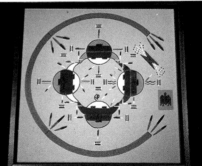

jewelers are masters at inlaying tiny-cut stones on bracelets and necklaces. The Navajo are renowned for their turquoise-and-silver jewelry and their beautifully woven rugs and blankets.

Today, the state's many jewelers, weavers, ceramicists, muralists, and struggling artists are evidence that the visual arts continue to thrive in New Mexico. R.C. Gorman, the most prominent modern Navajo artist, owns a gallery in Santa Fe.

A New Mexico artist works on a painting of the mountains near Santa Fe.

Countless galleries in Taos, Santa Fe, and other cities indicate that there is something magical about New Mexico that drives people to create.

ARCHITECTURE

In New Mexico, the word "pueblo" is used to describe a group of people, a town, or an architectural style. Pueblo architecture is a pleasant blend of Spanish and Indian building techniques. A typical pueblo house has a flat roof, thick walls, and protruding roofbeams that thrust through the front and back walls. With their smooth, flowing lines, pueblo houses merge naturally with the landscape and sometimes seem as much a part of the earth as one of New Mexico's many flat-topped mesas.

Pueblo houses originated when the Spaniards introduced sun-dried bricks, which they called *adobe*, to the Southwest. The Pueblo people, who for years had built dwellings out of mud and stone, learned quickly to use adobe bricks, and pueblo adobe houses soon began to appear throughout the state.

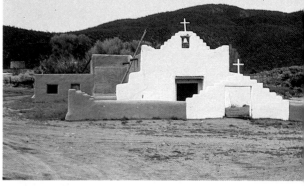

The pueblo style of architecture, which can be seen in its traditional form at Taos Pueblo (top left), has also been adapted for use in churches (top right), single-family homes (middle right, above), and even commercial buildings (right).

The pueblo style extends to large buildings and churches. In New Mexico, even some shopping malls and movie theaters have a pueblo look. The buildings at the University of New Mexico at Albuquerque are a celebration of pueblo architecture. Pueblo buildings in Las Vegas, most of which were constructed in the last century, are famed for the intricate carvings cut into their wooden beams. Santa Fe's Palace of the Governors is a pueblo classic that dates back nearly four centuries. The mission churches at Las Trampas and at Ranchos de Taos rank among the finest pueblo churches in the Southwest.

LITERATURE AND FOLKLORE

One morning thousands of years ago, the Zuñi people awoke to find a row of cornstalks growing on their dance court. Although they had never before seen corn, they realized at once that it was a gift from Paiyatuma, the most generous of the gods. In the spirit of thanksgiving, young people danced around the cornstalks while the elders sang prayers. But the villagers soon tired, and instead of continuing to give thanks, they fell asleep in the shade. Seeing this, Paiyatuma decided the Zuñi were ungrateful and snatched away the corn. Years of famine and thirst followed. Finally, Zuñi elders sent a group of brave young men to the land of the gods to implore Paiyatuma to give back the corn. Paiyatuma, moved by the suffering of his people, returned the gift. Ever since, the Zuñi have been faithful to the gods, and corn is their staple food to this day.

Hundreds of folktales such as this have been passed down from generation to generation by the Indian people of New Mexico. The Spaniards also had a host of stories and legends that persisted through the years. New Mexico's rich literary tradition continued after the Americans arrived.

During the height of the so-called lawless era of the late 1800s, Lew Wallace served as territorial governor. During his tenure, Wallace found time to write the popular historical novel *Ben-Hur*. The book, first published in 1880, was made into a popular movie starring Charlton Heston in 1959.

In the early 1900s, archaeologist Adolph Bandelier studied

Indian ruins at the place where a national monument now bears his name. Using his knowledge of ancient Indian culture, Bandelier wrote *The Delight Makers,* an imaginative novel set in prehistoric America.

Art patron Mabel Dodge Luhan brought such writers as Mary Austin and D. H. Lawrence to the art colony at Taos. They discovered what visual artists had found earlier—that the serenity and unusual beauty of New Mexico triggers creativity. As Englishman D. H. Lawrence wrote, "In the magnificent fierce mornings of New Mexico one sprang awake, a new part of the soul woke up suddenly, and the old world gave way to the new."

Willa Cather's novel *Death Comes to the Archbishop,* published in 1927, told the story of Santa Fe's Archbishop Jean Lamy, whose tireless energy brought formal schooling to New Mexico. Oliver La Farge's novel *Laughing Boy,* which won the Pulitzer Prize in 1929, narrated the struggle of Navajos torn between the white man's world and their traditional ways. The plight of a New Mexican frontier family was portrayed in Conrad Richter's 1937 novel *The Sea of Grass.*

Native Americans have contributed to the literary scene of New Mexico as well. One of the more notable Native American writers is Lucy Tapahonso, a Navajo who has published three books of poetry.

Gifted writers, filmmakers, and journalists began establishing homes in Santa Fe in the 1970s and 1980s. They included playwright Neil Simon, children's author Judy Blume, movie director Steven Spielberg, and cartoonist Bill Mauldin. Playwright Mark Medoff, head of the Theater Arts Department at New Mexico State University at Las Cruces, wrote the play *Children of a Lesser God.* In 1987, the play was made into an award-winning movie.

A mariachi band in Santa Fe

PERFORMING ARTS

New Mexican writer Oliver La Farge, a great admirer of Indian culture, gave this advice about watching Pueblo dance ceremonies: "When you attend [a Pueblo dance] you will at first be a trifle bewildered by the sheer mass, then fascinated by the costumes, the color, the music. Shortly after this you will find the performance monotonous, the sun hot, the ground hard, the dust annoying. This is the point at which many people leave. If you stay on, *and if you keep quiet*, the rhythms of drum, song, and dance, the endlessly changing formations of the lines of dancers, the very heat and the dust, unite and take hold. You will realize slowly that what looked simple is complex, disciplined, sophisticated. You will forget yourself. The chances are then you will go away with that same odd, empty feeling which comes after absorbing any great work of art."

As in many cultures, Indian music and dance have a religious

The Santa Fe Opera is a beautiful open-air theater situated in the foothills of the Sangre de Christo Mountains.

purpose. Through the dance ceremony, the people attempt to communicate with the magnificent spirit world.

The Spanish brought solemn church music, folk music, and lively folk dances to New Mexico. The fandango, a bouncy square dance, was favored by the early settlers. The brassy and spirited mariachi bands of Mexico are an honored part of the state's Spanish musical heritage.

"All lonely people sing," wrote one historian of western American music, "and much of the cowboy's work is done in solitude." Anglo cowboys kept warm during cold nights on the open range by sitting around a campfire singing songs accompanied by a fiddle or a guitar. Usually, the person with the best voice sang while the others joined in on the chorus. One popular cowboy song honored a famous desperado:

> I'll sing you the true song of Billy the Kid,
> I'll sing of the desperate deeds that he did;
> Way out in New Mexico long, long ago,
> When a man's only chance was his old forty-four.

New Mexico's cultural sophistication is embodied in the world-famous Santa Fe Opera. Situated dramatically in the mountains outside the capital, the open-air opera house hosts operas, classical symphonies, and chamber music. When the opera's season opens in July, all of Santa Fe's hotels fill up and the town buzzes with excitement. The Santa Fe Chamber Music Festival, also part of Santa Fe's summer arts season, is held in the beautiful St. Francis Auditorium at the Museum of Fine Arts. High-quality theater productions are presented by the Santa Fe Festival Theater and the British American Theatre Institute.

VIVA LA FIESTA!

Everyone loves a party, but New Mexicans take this love a few steps further than the average American. Their celebrations are thrown by entire towns, and sometimes draw people from all over the country.

Amid great pageantry and color, the Inter-Tribal Indian Ceremonial is held every August at Red Rock State Park near Gallup. The cultures of many tribes are displayed through dances, a rodeo, and art exhibits. One of the most fascinating of all Indian ceremonies is the Eagle Dance at Santa Clara Pueblo. The performers in this July event wear eagle costumes that are so authentic, one wonders when the dancers will soar off the ground.

The Wild West era is celebrated in southeastern New Mexico. In June, Fort Sumner hosts Old Fort Days, which feature a Tombstone Race, a Billy the Kid Outlaw Run, and Pat Garrett's Law and Order Swim Competition. Other pioneer-day fairs are held at Clovis, Ruidoso, and a number of other southeastern towns.

The Fiesta de Santa Fe, held in September, is perhaps the greatest New Mexican festival of all. It begins with the nighttime burning of a huge wooden figure, called Zozobra, that is meant to symbolize Old Man Gloom. With Gloom lying in ashes, Joy is

The Inter-Tribal Indian Ceremonial is held every August at
Red Rock State Park near Gallup.

born, and the ancient Plaza explodes with mariachi music. The
fiesta lasts three days or until everyone is exhausted—whichever
comes first.

Fiestas, of course, go hand in hand with food. Those unfamiliar
with New Mexican food must beware because the dishes are often
seasoned with fiery chile peppers. The first bite sets one's mouth
afire. Soon, however, the delectable flavor drowns out the wrath
of the pepper. Many travelers hail New Mexico as the home of the
country's greatest cuisine. An interesting side dish that originated
in the American Southwest is puffy, deep-fried bread called
sopaipilla. Served hot and with honey, sopaipilla is tantalizing.

Despite the delicious Spanish-based food of New Mexico, it is
difficult to satisfy everyone. Anglo cowboys who camped out on
the range often became tired of beans, Spanish New Mexico's
staple food. A chorus in one cowboy song went:

> Oh, It's bacon and beans
> Most every day.
> I'd sooner be eatin'
> Prairie hay.

93

Chapter 10
HIGHLIGHTS OF THE LAND OF ENCHANTMENT

HIGHLIGHTS OF THE LAND OF ENCHANTMENT

Each year, some 22.6 million travelers come to New Mexico. They tour the state's lively cities, gaze with awe at its countryside, and explore the ruins of its wondrous ancient civilizations.

THE NORTHEAST

Two branches of the Santa Fe Trail once passed through the northeast part of the state. Because of the dry climate, one can still detect a few hundred-year-old ruts left by traders' wagons. The Santa Fe Trail Museum in the town of Springer and nearby Fort Union National Monument tell the story of this famous roadway.

Las Vegas, New Mexico has an honored role in state history. It was there, during the Mexican War in 1846, that General Stephen Watts Kearny first declared New Mexico a part of the United States.

Cimarron was once known as the cowboy capital of the world. Some of the Old West's most famous names, including Kit Carson and "Buffalo Bill" Cody, lived there for brief periods. It was one of the most lawless towns in a lawless era, as this line from the *Las Vegas Gazette* illustrates: "Everything is quiet in Cimarron. Nobody has been killed in three days. . . ." Another cattle town, Tucumcari, has contributed to today's impressions of how the Old West looked. The 1950s hit television series "Rawhide," starring a youthful Clint Eastwood, was filmed there.

Fort Union
National Monument

Ghost towns are communities that sprang up around a mine or railroad, but were abandoned once the source of income was depleted. Today, the weatherbeaten ruins of a number of ghost towns beckon to the curious traveler. One survey reports that there are as many as 130 ghost towns in New Mexico.

Colfax, which lies twenty-eight miles (forty-five kilometers) southwest of Raton, has been a ghost town since the Great Depression. A victim of poor planning, the town was built at a spot too far from popular crossroads. Gradually, its citizens packed up and moved to more-prosperous locales. In the center of Colfax, a forlorn-looking frame hotel stands to remind visitors of its more promising days.

THE SOUTHEAST

The southeast region of the state is known as "Little Texas" because many of its residents are recent immigrants from New Mexico's southeastern neighbor. As in Texas, oil has contributed to the area's development. Located near oil fields, the towns of Hobbs and Lovington were both prosperous in the late 1970s when oil prices soared, but experienced economic depression in the 1980s when the price of oil dropped.

Roswell, the state's fourth-largest city, lies in the heart of southeastern New Mexico. It began in 1869, when a professional

Carlsbad Caverns in southeastern New Mexico

gambler established a lone store on a cattle trail and named the area after his father, Roswell Smith. The Roswell Museum and Art Center houses the memorabilia of Robert H. Goddard, the father of modern rocketry. The International Space Hall of Fame in Alamogordo, which celebrates the results of Goddard's dreams, contains moon rocks, model space stations, and exhibits that salute American space pioneers.

Astonishing Carlsbad Caverns is the region's most popular attraction. This vast maze of caves was formed two hundred million years ago, when the Rocky Mountains were mere foothills. Although the ancient Basketmakers once lived in the caverns, their modern discovery is credited to a cowboy named Jim White, who stumbled across the entrance in 1901. At the time, White was following the flight of a huge swarm of bats. Today, tens of thousands of bats still live in Carlsbad Caverns.

Every day, hundreds of visitors venture into the caverns and pass through forests of stalactites and stalagmites that stand like great, stony icicles. Tourists are overwhelmed by the scope of Big Room, which is more than ten football fields long and about twenty-two stories high. Signs point out such smaller rock formations as Whale's Mouth and Baby Hippo, which look curiously like their namesakes. Tours of Carlsbad Caverns show only a tiny part of this natural wonder. The complex beehive of caves runs endless miles through the limestone, and many caverns remain unexplored.

NORTH-CENTRAL NEW MEXICO

The north is the historic heartland of the rural, old-line Hispanics. In dusty villages such as Truchas, Chimayó, and Coyote, some descendants of the Spanish conquistadores still speak a form of sixteenth-century Spanish used nowhere else in the world.

With more than sixty art galleries, a music school, and more than a dozen historic sites, the city of Taos remains a cultural mecca. Settled by Spaniards in 1615, Taos is one of the oldest European communities in the United States. In a nearby cemetery rest two of the town's most famous citizens—frontiersman Kit Carson and art patron Mabel Dodge Luhan.

Taos Pueblo, which stands 2 miles (3.2 kilometers) north of the city of Taos, is one of the oldest continously occupied communities in the United States. How old is Taos Pueblo? It was a lively town when Europe was mired in the Dark Ages. Its two main buildings are nine-hundred-years old, and residents still live comfortably within their walls.

History and rugged hiking meet at Bandelier National Monument. Bandelier's 50 square miles (129.5 square kilometers) of forested parklands contain dozens of ancient Indian sites. Some lie a few feet from the Visitors' Center, while others can be reached only by those willing to hike ten miles (sixteen kilometers) or more through Bandelier's beautiful wilderness. The nearby Puyé Cliff Dwellings hold still more ancient "apartment houses."

Above: Albuquerque at night
Right: a downtown mall in Albuquerque

ALBUQUERQUE AND SANTA FE

Almost in the shadow of Albuquerque's high-rise office buildings lies Old Town Plaza. The Old Town area was the original heart of Albuquerque when it was founded in 1706 as a Spanish farming community. The village was named after a province in Spain that was ruled by a duke, and today it retains the nickname "Duke City." Its history is well displayed at the Albuquerque Museum of Art, History, and Science, located at the edge of Old Town. The National Atomic Museum, which features exhibits tracing the development of atomic energy and the atomic bomb, is both fascinating and frightening. Albuquerque's Indian Pueblo Culture Center is a fine place to study the subtle differences in Pueblo art; each of the nineteen Pueblo groups has a separate exhibit there. Albuquerque also boasts the Rio Grande Zoo, where most animals are in surroundings that resemble their natural habitats. The University of New Mexico at Albuquerque is an architectural gem of the pueblo style.

Every year in August, the Santa Fe Plaza (above) becomes the site of an Indian Market (left), where more than three hundred Navajo and Pueblo exhibitors display contemporary and traditional artwork.

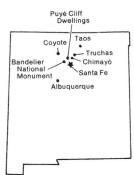

Since World War II, Albuquerque's population has grown tenfold. Its metropolitan area topped the one-half-million mark in 1988—and the growth of Albuquerque continues. As Mayor Ken Schultz said in 1987, "Albuquerque is on the edge of greatness."

New Mexico's heart and soul begins at the Plaza of Santa Fe. Almost every day, Indian artisans dressed in traditional clothing sit along the Plaza's wall selling jewelry, rugs, pottery, and other handcrafts. At one corner of the Plaza is the End of the Trail Monument, a plaque that honors the hardy travelers who reached the destination point of the famed 800-mile (1,287-kilometer) Santa Fe Trail. On one side of the Plaza is the nearly four-hundred-year-old Palace of the Governors, which served as the residence and office of New Mexico's territorial governors. Today, the sprawling adobe stucture houses a museum devoted to the cultural history of New Mexico and the Southwest. Next door is the Museum of Fine Arts, housed in a beautiful pueblo-style building and featuring an outstanding collection of southwestern art. A short distance from the Plaza stands the circular State Capitol Building.

The foundation of Santa Fe's Chapel of San Miguel was laid in 1610, making it one of the oldest churches in the United States. Nearby Loretto Chapel was completed without a staircase to the choir loft after its architect was killed in an 1873 pistol duel. Shortly after, a mysterious stranger appeared, built a beautiful wooden staircase without nails, and then disappeared, leaving no bill, name, or address. Scholars who analyzed the wood determined that it could not have come from this continent. Legend says that the mysterious man was St. Joseph, who was a carpenter by trade.

Santa Fe is called "the city different," and that difference can be seen in the often unusual entertainers who roam the streets. One, known as the Rubber Lady, dresses in an otherworldly latex costume. Children follow her wherever she goes, but no one knows her name. Clowns, mimes, or puppeteers pop up unannounced and entertain the people sitting on benches in the Plaza. On weekend nights, the "low riders," whose cars sit so low that the bumpers almost scrape the pavement, crawl through the streets. A visiting student reflecting on this pleasant madness wrote home, "Santa Fe is a city that celebrates itself."

SOUTH-CENTRAL NEW MEXICO

The state's startling contrasts are seen dramatically in the south-central region. A mere ten-minute drive takes one from the forests

102

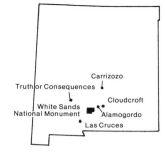

White Sands National Monument is
a desert of gleaming white gypsum
sand in south-central New Mexico.

of the Sacramento Mountains near Cloudcroft, to a desert so
blazing white that people must shield their eyes from the glare.

Spreading over 144,000 acres (58,277 hectares), the parklands of
White Sands National Monument attract thousands of visitors
each year. This unique desert is composed of gypsum crystals
instead of sand. Its glistening dunes are so white that at dusk they
resemble deep fields of sparkling snow.

North of White Sands National Monument, a small placard
marks Trinity Site, where, in 1945, the world's first atomic bomb
was detonated. Centuries ago, the Spaniards gave the wasteland
adjacent to Trinity Site a nickname that rings with bitter irony:
Jornada del Muerto (Journey of the Dead).

The city of Truth or Consequences was once called Hot Springs
and was famed for its mineral baths. In 1950, the town changed its
name to the title of a popular radio quiz program. At first, the
gimmicky name drew tourists to the community, but today when
someone says "I am from Truth or Consequences," people from
outside New Mexico look at him and say, "What?"

White Oaks is a ghost town northeast of Carrizozo. In the late
1800s, the town prospered from the activities of a nearby gold
mine. It boasted a thousand residents and two newspapers. But
the gold ran out, the railroads bypassed White Oaks, and the town
has been virtually deserted since the 1930s.

Far from being a ghost town is Las Cruces, the state's third-largest city and the home of New Mexico State University. Las Cruces lies in the heart of the rich Mesilla Valley, where farmers grow onions, pecans, and the state's most popular spice—chile peppers. The city's name, which is Spanish for "the crosses," has an unusual origin. In the mid-1800s, Indians attacked a Spanish caravan at the place where the town now stands, and many people were killed. The victims were buried on the spot, and the town eventually grew up around the dozens of crosses that marked their graves.

NORTHWESTERN NEW MEXICO

Almost three-fourths of the state's Indian population live in the northwest. The region contains the huge Navajo Reservation, the Jicarilla Apache Reservation, and the Zuñi Reservation. In the distant past, the northwestern region was the home of the fascinating Anasazi people.

Salmon Ruins, Aztec Ruins National Monument, and Chaco Culture National Historical Park are spellbinding Anasazi sites. Since the late 1970s, when excavation began at Salmon Ruins near Bloomfield, 1.5 million artifacts ranging from pottery shards to elegant vases have been unearthed. Pueblo Bonito at Chaco Culture National Historic Park is the most incredible of all of the state's ancient ruins. A thousand years ago, it was a single building that rose five stories and contained eight hundred rooms. Today its walls still stand, a monument to the great Anasazi builders.

One of the state's most famous rock formations is the towering volcanic mountain known as Shiprock. Some say it is shaped like a ship with full-blown sails. According to Navajo legend,

The San Juan River (right) runs through Farmington (above),
the largest city in northwestern New Mexico.

Shiprock was once the home of a prehistoric giant bird that
preyed on the Navajos for food for its young.

Farmington is northwestern New Mexico's largest city. The
mining and processing of oil, gas, and coal are its major
industries. Winding through the city is the lazy San Juan River.
Forty miles (sixty-four kilometers) east of Farmington, the river
flows into Navajo Lake, a popular spot for boating, waterskiing,
and fishing.

Gallup, which calls itself the "Indian Capital of the World,"
serves as a trading center for more than twenty different Indian
groups. Every August, Gallup is the site of the Inter-Tribal Indian
Ceremonial.

The Zuñi Reservation is the farthest west of New Mexico's
nineteen pueblos. Zuñi Pueblo is famed for its *Shalako* ceremony,
an exotic, all-night tribute to giant gods that takes place in late

Gila National Monument
Mogollon
Gila Wilderness
Silver City
City of Rocks State Park
Coronado National Forest

The Gila National Forest is the largest national forest in the United States.

November. To the east of Zuñi Pueblo is the Pueblo "Sky City" of Acoma, built eight hundred years ago on top of a tall mesa.

Returning from an expedition that had reached the Gulf of California, a group of early Spaniards carved a message on the side of a sandstone mesa that they named El Morro. Travelers who followed continued to leave inscriptions to mark their passage through the region, thus giving the landmark its other name: Inscription Rock. The words of the original message, which can still be read, proclaim in Spanish: "Passed by here the Governor Don Juan de Oñate from the discovery of the Sea of the South on the sixteenth of April, 1605."

THE SOUTHWEST

Gold, silver, and dreams of overnight riches spurred the development of southwestern New Mexico. Silver City grew from a tiny Spanish settlement into a midsized town because of the rich mines lying nearby. Today, ranching and copper mining have helped Silver City remain a vibrant town. Many of its sister communities, however, died long ago. Southwestern New Mexico is an intriguing graveyard of ghost towns.

Mogollon, 75 miles (121 kilometers) northwest of Silver City, once produced nearly $20 million in gold, held 1,800 inhabitants, and supported 22 saloons. At one time, it was the hangout of notorious western badman Butch Cassidy. But a devastating series of fires and floods, combined with the exhaustion of its gold fields, turned Mogollon into a ghost town. Other interesting abandoned towns in the area are Chloride, Kelly, Shakespeare, and Steins.

Spreading over 3.3 million acres (1.3 million hectares), the Gila National Forest is the nation's largest national forest. It includes the Gila Wilderness, the first area to be set aside by Congress as a national wilderness area. The wonders of Gila Wilderness can be experienced only by the rugged. No roads pierce its interior, and visitors must enter the deep forest by horseback or on foot. Much of the Gila National Forest has never been touched by an ax, and its mule deer are so fearless that one can almost get close enough to touch them.

Far to the south lies New Mexico's "Boot Heel," a stub of land that dips into Mexico. Coronado National Forest is the highlight of this sparsely populated region. City of Rocks State Park features unusual rock formations that resemble clusters of tall buildings. Running along the tip of the boot heel is the Mexican border, which serves as a reminder of the state's ancient ties with Mexico and its priceless Spanish heritage.

Visitors to New Mexico can't help but be enchanted by the state's dramatic beauty and vibrant mix of cultures. When asked to describe the almost mystical lure of New Mexico, writer Oliver La Farge said, "[It is] a land that draws and holds men and women with ties that cannot be explained or submitted to reason."

FACTS AT A GLANCE

GENERAL INFORMATION

Statehood: January 6, 1912, forty-seventh state

Origin of Name: New Mexico was named by sixteenth-century Spanish explorers who hoped to find gold and wealth equal to Mexico's Aztec treasures

State Capital: Santa Fe

State Nickname: The "Land of Enchantment"

State Flag: New Mexico has had two official state flags. The first, adopted in 1915, consisted of a blue field with the United States flag in the upper left corner, the number "47" (identifying New Mexico as the forty-seventh state) in the upper right corner, the state seal in the lower right corner, and the words "New Mexico" written across the field from lower left to upper right. The present state flag, adopted in 1925, displays the ancient sun symbol of the Zia Pueblo in red against a field of yellow. The Zia Sun Symbol is a circle from which four points radiate. The circle symbolizes life and love, which, according to the Zias, are without beginning and end. The number four, sacred to the Zias, symbolizes the four directions, the four seasons of the year, the four periods of the day (sunrise, noon, evening, and night), and the four divisions in human life (childhood, youth, adulthood, and old age). Red and yellow were the colors of the Spanish conquistadores.

State Motto: *Crescit Eundo,* "It Grows as It Goes"

State Bird: Roadrunner

State Animal: Black bear

State Fish: Cutthroat trout

State Flower: Yucca flower

State Tree: Piñon (nut pine)

State Gem: Turquoise

State Vegetable: Chile pepper and frijole (pinto bean)

State Song: New Mexico has two state songs. "O Fair New Mexico," words and music by Elizabeth Garrett, was adopted in 1917. "Así Es Nuevo Méjico," words and music by Amadeo Lucero, was adopted in 1971.

O FAIR NEW MEXICO

Under a sky of azure, where balmy breezes blow,
Kissed by the golden sunshine, is Nuevo Mejico.
Home of the Montezuma, with fiery heart aglow,
State of the deeds historic, is Nuevo Mejico.

Chorus:
O, fair New Mexico, we love, we love you so,
Our hearts with pride o'erflow, no matter where
   we go,
O, fair New Mexico, we love you, we love you so,
The grandest state to know, New Mexico.

Rugged and high sierras, with deep canyons below,
Dotted with fertile valleys, is Nuevo Mejico.
Fields full of sweet alfalfa, richest perfumes
   bestow,
State of apple blossoms, is Nuevo Mejico.

(Chorus)

Days that are full of heart-dreams, nights when the
   moon hangs low,
Beaming its benediction, o'er Nuevo Mejico.
Land with its bright *mañana*, coming through weal
   and woe,
State of our *esperanza*, is Nuevo Mejico.

ASÍ ES NUEVO MÉJICO

Un canto que traigo muy dentro del alma
Lo canto a mi estado, mi tierra natal.
De flores dorada mi tierra encantada
De lindas mujeres, que no tiene igual.

Chorus:
Así es Nuevo Méjico
Así es esta tierra del sol
De sierras y valles de tierras frutales
Así es Nuevo Méjico.

El negro, el hispano, el anglo, y el indio,
Todos son tus hijos, todos por igual.
Tus pueblos, y aldeas, mi tierra encantada
De lindas mujeres que no tiene igual.

(Chorus)

El Río del Norte que es el Río Grande
Sus aguas corrientes fluyen hasta el mar,
Y riegan tus campos
Mi tierra encantada de lindas mujeres
Que no tiene igual.

(Chorus)

Tus campos se visten de flores de Mayo,
De lindos colores
Que Dios les doto
Tus pajaros cantan mi tierra encantada
Sus trinos de amores
Al ser celestial.

(Chorus)

Mi tierra encantada de historia banada
Tan linda, tan bella, sin comparacion.
Te rindo homenaje, te rindo carino
Soldado valiente, te rinde su amor.

POPULATION

Population: 1,303,445, thirty-seventh among the states (1980 census)

Population Density: 11 people per sq. mi. (4 people per km²)

Population Distribution: 72 percent of the people live in cities or towns. About 33 percent of New Mexico's total population live in the Albuquerque metropolitan area alone.

Albuquerque	331,767
Santa Fe	48,953
Las Cruces	45,086
Roswell	39,679
Farmington	3i,222
Clovis	31,194
Hobbs	29,153
Carlsbad	25,496
Gallup	18,167

(Population figures according to 1980 census)

Population Growth: Native Americans have been living in New Mexico for some twenty thousand years. The Pueblo, Apache, Comanche, Navajo, and Ute peoples were in the New Mexico region when Spanish settlers arrived in the 1600s. Anglos (non-Spanish white Americans) began to arrive slowly but steadily during the American territorial period, which began in 1850. New Mexico's greatest population increase came after 1940, when workers from all over the country flocked to the state for jobs in atomic-energy research at White Sands and Los Alamos. From 1940 to 1960, the state's population nearly doubled. From 1970 to 1980, New Mexico's population grew 28 percent, while the population of the entire country grew 11.45 percent. The list below shows population growth in New Mexico since 1880:

Year	Population
1880	119,565
1900	195,310
1920	360,350
1940	531,818
1960	951,023
1970	1,016,000
1980	1,303,445

GEOGRAPHY

Borders: States that border New Mexico are Colorado on the north, Oklahoma on the east, Texas on the east and south, Arizona on the west, and Utah at the northwest corner. Mexico forms part of New Mexico's southern border.

Highest Point: Wheeler Peak in Taos County, 13,161 ft. (4,011 m)

Lowest Point: Red Bluff Reservoir in Eddy County, 2,817 ft. (859 m)

Greatest Distances: North to south—391 mi. (629 km)
East to west—353 mi. (566 km)

Area: 121,593 sq. mi. (314,938 km^2)

Rank in Area Among the States: Fifth

Indian Reservations: Ten percent, or more than 8 million acres (3.2 million hectares) of New Mexico's land is Indian land. The largest portion of this land (4.8 million acres/1.9 million hectares) is Navajo land. The Navajo Reservation occupies parts of Socorro, Bernalillo, Sandoval, Valencia, San Juan, and McKinley counties. New Mexico's nineteen Pueblo groups occupy 1.9 million acres (.76 million hectares) of land. The Laguna and Zuñi pueblos are the largest; Sandia Pueblo is the smallest. The Jicarilla Apache Reservation lies in northern New Mexico; the Mescalero Apache Reservation lies in south-central New Mexico. The large Ute Mountain Reservation extends over parts of both New Mexico and Colorado, with most of the population living on the Colorado side.

Sandstone cliffs in the Jemez Range

Rivers: The Rio Grande, also known as the Rio Bravo or the "Great River," is New Mexico's longest river. It flows through the state from north to south and forms part of the state's southern border with Texas. From its origin in the mountains of Colorado to its mouth at the Gulf of Mexico, the Rio Grande stretches 1,800 mi. (2,896 km). Its principal New Mexico tributaries are the Jemez, Chama, and Red rivers. The Canadian River rises in the northeast and flows eastward into Oklahoma, where it joins the Arkansas River. The Pecos River rises in the Sangre de Cristo Mountains and flows in a southeasterly direction into Texas, where it joins the Rio Grande. West of the Continental Divide, the Gila and San Juan rivers flow westward out of the state to join the Colorado River.

Lakes: New Mexico's largest lakes were created artificially to provide water for irrigation. Elephant Butte Reservoir (62.5 sq. mi./162 km^2) and Conchas Reservoir (25 sq. mi./64.8 km^2) are by far the largest. Other important reservoirs are Abiquiu, Avalon, Bluewater, Eagle Nest, El Vado, McMillan, Navajo, and Sumner. The Bottomless Lakes, a group of deep pools near Roswell, are the state's best-known natural lakes.

Topography: New Mexico's land can be divided into four topographical regions: the Great Plains, the Rocky Mountains, the Colorado Plateau, and the Basin and Range Region. The Continental Divide snakes through the state from north to south in the western third of the state. Rivers east of the divide drain into the Gulf of Mexico; rivers west of the divide drain into the Pacific Ocean.

113

The eastern third of the state is dominated by the Great Plains. Some of New Mexico's major oil and gas fields are located in this region. The northern, or Raton section of the plains, is a high, rugged plateau, where deep canyons have been slashed by the Canadian River and its tributaries. The southern section of the Great Plains includes the broad Pecos River Valley, which supports dry farming. East of the Pecos and south of the Canadian River is the flat, river-formed, *Llano Estacado* (Staked Plain) section of the Great Plains.

The Rocky Mountains, which extend south from the state's northern border to the Santa Fe area, cover north-central New Mexico. The Rio Grande threads its way south through this region. East of the Rio Grande are the Sangre de Cristo Mountains, which include Wheeler Peak, New Mexico's highest point. To the west are the Nacimiento and Jemez ranges.

The Colorado Plateau occupies New Mexico's northwestern corner. Rich oil and gas fields and uranium deposits are found here. The region is a broken country of buttes, rugged mesas, dry washes, and extensive lava plains. The San Juan River forms a broad, fertile valley on its course westward through the plateau.

The Basin and Range Region, in the southwestern and central part of the state, covers roughly one-third of New Mexico. This area is characterized by isolated mountain ranges, including the Sandia, Manzano, San Andres, Sacramento, Caballos, Magdalena, Mimbres, San Mateo, Black, and Mogollon ranges. The mountains are separated by low, broad, desert basins, such as the Tularosa and Jornada del Muerto. The fertile valley and irrigated farmlands along the Rio Grande make this one of the state's richest agricultural areas.

Climate: New Mexico's climate is warm and dry. The state is known for its plentiful sunshine and low humidity. Summer temperatures are high in the daytime, but cool at night. July temperatures average 65°F. (18°C) in the northern part of the state and 80°F. (27°C) in the south. In some places, the temperature may reach 90°F. (32°C) or more on a sunny day, and yet drop to 50°F. (10°C) at night. Although winter months may bring below-freezing temperatures in most parts of the state, January temperatures average 35°F. (2°C) in the north and 55°F. (13°C) in the south. The state's highest recorded temperature was 116°F. (47°C) at Artesia on June 29, 1918 and at Orogrande on July 14, 1934; the lowest recorded temperature was -50°F. (-45°C) at Gavilan on February 1, 1951.

Annual precipitation (rain and snow) averages 20 in. (50 cm), per year, but varies widely from region to region. The southwestern deserts may experience as little as 8 in. (20 cm) of precipitation per year, including about 2 in. (5 cm) of winter snow. Albuquerque, in north-central New Mexico, averages 10 in. (25 cm) of annual snowfall. The northern mountains may be buried under 300 in. (762 cm) of snow in the winter. In the summer, thunderstorms are common throughout the state. About one-half of the annual rainfall occurs between June and August.

NATURE

Trees: Aspens, cedars, cottonwoods, Douglas firs, white firs, junipers, piñons, ponderosa pine and other pines, oaks, shrub live oaks, and spruces are typical forest trees. Shrubs include blackbrush, creosote bush, manzanita, mesquite, sagebrush, sumac, and tarbush.

Wild Plants: Asters, cacti, coneflowers, fireweed, forget-me-nots, grasses, larkspurs, locoweed, lupines, penstemons, sages, saxifrages, sedges, soapweed, and yucca are among the most common wild plants.

Animals: Pronghorn antelope, badgers, beavers, black bears, bobcats, chipmunks, coyotes, deer, elk, foxes, javelinas, mountain lions, lizards, minks, otters, raccoons, foxes, prairie dogs, jackrabbits, bighorn sheep, rattlesnakes, coral snakes

Birds: Some 432 species of birds can be found in New Mexico, including crows, doves, ducks, finches, grouse, hummingbirds, jays, meadowlarks, orioles, pheasants, quail, ravens, roadrunners, shrikes, starlings, swallows, swifts, thrashers, thrushes, wild turkeys, vireos, warblers, waxwings, woodpeckers, and wrens.

Fish: Black and largemouth bass, catfish, crappies, perch, suckers, northern pike, trout

GOVERNMENT

The government of New Mexico, like that of the federal government, is divided into three branches: executive, legislative, and judicial. The state legislature, elected by the voters, is responsible for making the laws. It consists of a seventy-member house and a forty-two member senate. State senators serve four-year terms and state representatives serve two-year terms. The legislature meets annually in January for sixty-day terms in odd numbered years and thirty-day terms in even-numbered years.

The executive branch, headed by the governor, is responsible for administering the law. The governor is elected to a four-year-term and may serve no more than two consecutive terms. The governor has the power to veto legislation passed by the state legislature and to appoint most of the directors and board members of state agencies.

The judicial branch interprets the law and tries cases. The state's highest court is the supreme court, which has five justices. Each justice is elected by the voters to an eight-year term; the terms are staggered so that a totally new court cannot be elected during one election. The justices of the supreme court elect their own chief justice every two years. The court of appeals, which hears appeals from the district courts, has seven justices who are elected to eight-year terms. The state's principal trial courts are the district courts. There are fifty-seven district court judges; they are elected from thirteen judicial districts and serve six-year terms. In addition, the state has magistrate, metropolitan, and probate courts.

Number of Counties: 33

U.S. Representatives: 3

Electoral Votes: 5

Chile peppers hanging out to dry

EDUCATION

Public education in New Mexico is administered through eighty-nine local school districts under the direction of ten elected and five governor-appointed members of the State Board of Education. New Mexico has about 400 public elementary schools and 211 public junior and senior high schools. Each year, the state spends about $2,901 per student. Total public-school enrollment is about 270,000 students. An additional 20,000 students attend private schools.

The University of New Mexico at Albuquerque is the state's largest university, with an enrollment of about 24,000 students. About 13,000 students are enrolled at New Mexico State University in Las Cruces. Other state universities include Eastern New Mexico University in Portales, New Mexico Highlands University in Las Vegas, Western New Mexico University in Silver City, and New Mexico Institute of Mining and Technology in Socorro. Private schools include College of Santa Fe, College of the Southwest in Hobbs, St. John's College in Santa Fe, San Juan College in Farmington, and Navajo Community College in Shiprock.

ECONOMY AND INDUSTRY

Principal Products:

Agriculture: Beef cattle, sheep, milk, cotton, hay, wheat, corn, sorghum grain, pecans, onions, alfalfa, apples, barley, cantaloupes, chile peppers, pinto beans, grapes, hogs, lettuce, oats, potatoes, poultry, peanuts, sweet potatoes, tomatoes

Manufacturing: Processed food, electrical machinery and equipment, nuclear products, printed materials, lumber and wood products, glass products, clothing, aircraft parts, plastics, petroleum and coal products, computer chips

Natural Resources: Uranium, natural gas, petroleum, potash, gypsum, coal, clays, copper, gold, silver, iron, molybdenum, pumice, helium gas, perlite, salt, stone, zinc, sand and gravel, lead, manganese, mica, forests

Business and Trade: Federal government research centers, such as Sandia National Laboratories at Kirtland Air Force Base near Albuquerque, White Sands Missile Range in south-central New Mexico, and the weapons development center at Los Alamos, contribute a great deal to the state's economy. In fact, government, which employs 25 percent of New Mexico's working population, is the state's most important industry. More than 130,000 New Mexicans are employed by various government agencies.

Food processing is the major manufacturing activity in the state. The mining of New Mexico's rich reserves of minerals, including oil, natural gas, copper, coal, potash, and uranium, is another important economic activity in the state. Mining contributes about $6 billion a year to the state's economy. A recent major development has been the growth of industrial parks, especially in the Albuquerque area. New Mexico's natural beauty and variety of cultures has made both filmmaking and tourism important industries in the state.

Communication: The state has about ninety-six radio stations and twelve television stations. Albuquerque, the state's largest city, has thirty-nine radio stations and receives four television stations. The state's largest newspapers are the *Albuquerque Journal*, the *Albuquerque Tribune*, the *Las Cruces Sun News*, and the *New Mexican* in Santa Fe. Other papers of note include the *Alamogordo Daily News*, the *Current Argus* in Carlsbad, the *Farmington Daily Times*, the *Gallup Independent*, the *Hobbs Daily News*, the *Los Alamos Monitor*, and the *Roswell Daily Record*. In all, New Mexico has about fifty newspapers, including about twenty dailies. The weekly *Navajo Times* is the only Navajo-owned and operated newspaper in the United States.

Transportation: There are about 70,000 mi. (112,000 km) of roads and highways in New Mexico, of which approximately 15,000 mi. (24,100 km) are paved. Three interstate highways cross the state. Interstate Highway 40 is an east-west route running through the center of the state, Interstate 25 runs north-south from Raton to Las Cruces, and Interstate 10 runs east-west in the southern part of the state. New Mexico has approximately eighty public and sixty private airports. The largest is Albuquerque International Airport, which is served by about ten national airlines, two regional airlines, and five commuter airlines. New Mexico has about 2,200 mi. (3,540 km) of railroad track. Five railroads provide freight and passenger service. Both the Southern Pacific and Santa Fe railroads cross the state. Albuquerque is an important stop on the Chicago-Los Angeles Amtrak route.

SOCIAL AND CULTURAL LIFE

Museums: New Mexico has many fine museums, several of which are in Santa Fe. Santa Fe's Museum of International Folk Art has one of the world's largest collections of international folk art. The Museum of Fine Arts houses an extensive collection of paintings, photography, drawings, and sculptures by southwestern and New Mexican artists. The Laboratory of Anthropology/Museum of Indian Art and Culture is noted for its outstanding collection of Indian arts, crafts, and artifacts. The Palace of the Governors, which has been in continuous use since 1610, is now a museum that has exhibits of New Mexico history. The Wheelwright Museum contains a fine collection of Navajo ceremonial art, and the museum of the Institute of American Arts features contemporary works by Native Americans.

In Albuquerque, the Albuquerque Museum explores more than four hundred years of New Mexico history. Exhibits on paleontology, geology, biology, and other fields of natural history are featured at the Museum of Natural History. The Fine Arts Museum has many contemporary works of art. The Maxwell Museum of Anthropology contains outstanding exhibits of prehistoric and historic Indian cultures. The Indian Pueblo Cultural Center features the arts and crafts of the various New Mexico Pueblos. The National Atomic Museum on Kirtland Air Force Base has exhibits outlining the development of nuclear energy and atomic weapons. In Los Alamos, one can visit the Bradbury Science Hall and Museum, which features nuclear energy and physics exhibits; and the County Historical Museum, which presents the history of the Manhattan Project.

Libraries: The New Mexico State Library has six regional offices and assists the more than one hundred libraries throughout the state. The Albuquerque Public Library, with eight branches, two bookmobiles, and more than 1.7 million volumes, is the state's largest public library. The University of New Mexico, with more than 1.2 million volumes, is the state's largest academic library.

Performing Arts: The Santa Fe Opera, located in a beautiful, open-air theater in the foothills of the Sangre de Christo Mountains, is one of America's most respected musical organizations. Its immensely popular summer season, which draws music-lovers from all over the world, has presented more than thirty world or American premieres of important musical works. The Santa Fe Chamber Music Festival, also held in the summer, features a six-week series of chamber music concerts performed by highly acclaimed musical artists. Summer chamber music concerts are also presented by the Taos School of Music. The Santa Fe Symphony Orchestra performs five times a year at the Sweeney Convention Center. Since 1974, the Orchestra of Santa Fe has performed at the Lensic Theater. The Santa Fe Desert Chorale performs a wide range of choral music. The Santa Fe Concert Association sponsors a winter series that brings many of the world's leading musicians to Santa Fe. Las Cruces has a fine symphony orchestra.

Albuquerque also boasts a wide range of musical offerings. The New Mexico Symphony Orchestra, founded in 1934, performs at Popejoy Hall on the University of New Mexico campus. For many years, the renowned Guarneri String Quartet has been performing in Albuquerque as part of the June Music Festival. The ninety-member Albuquerque Civic Chorus performs at the Kimo theater. The La Zarzuela de Albuquerque features light operettas performed in Spanish.

Plays and musicals imported from Broadway and elsewhere are presented by the Albuquerque Civic Light Opera and at Popejoy Hall by touring companies. The New Mexico Repertory Theater performs Shakespeare and contemporary plays in both Albuquerque and Santa Fe. High-quality productions are also presented in Santa Fe by the Santa Fe Festival Theater, the British American Theatre Institute, and the Santa Fe Community Theater. Maria Benitez's Estampa Flamenca performs authentic Spanish flamenco dancing in Santa Fe during the summer months.

Sports and Recreation: New Mexico is not represented by teams in any of the major sports leagues. The Albuquerque Dukes (the AAA team of the Los Angeles

**The All-Indian
Rodeo in Gallup**

Dodgers), however, play in the excellent Pacific Coast Baseball League and have a loyal following. University and college football and basketball teams are also followed avidly by New Mexican sports fans. Rodeos, held at every county fair, are very popular. Horse racing is held at the downs at Santa Fe and Albuquerque, La Mesa Park in Raton, the New Mexico State Fair in Albuquerque, Ruidoso Downs in Ruidoso, San Juan Downs in Farmington, and Sunland Park near Las Cruces. The International Balloon Fiesta, the world's largest hot-air balloon rally, is held every October in Albuquerque.

New Mexico has seven national forests: Gila, Apache, Carson, Cibola (made up of several separate forests), Coronado, Lincoln, and Santa Fe. Parts of Coronado and Apache national forests lie in Arizona. New Mexico has nine national monuments, one national park (Carlsbad Caverns National Park), and more than forty state parks and monuments. These parklands offer everything from rugged wilderness areas to fascinating historic sites. Popular outdoor sports include backpacking and rock climbing in the mountains and wilderness areas; swimming, sailing, waterskiing, and canoeing on the state's lakes and streams; and, in the winter, snowmobiling, downhill and cross-country skiing, and ice fishing. Whitewater rafting can be done at a number of points along the Rio Grande. New Mexico's many rivers and streams can be fished for largemouth bass, northern pike, walleye, crappie, and trout. Antelope, elk, bears, javelinas, turkeys, whitetailed deer, mule deer, and such exotic animals as Persian ibex, barbary sheep, bighorn sheep, and oryx may (with a proper permit) be hunted in the mountains and plains.

Historic Sites and Landmarks:

Aztec Ruins National Monument, north of Aztec, preserves the ruins of an Anasazi pueblo that thrived in the 1100s. The Great Kiva (underground ceremonial chamber) used by the early pueblo dwellers has been excavated and fully restored.

Bandelier National Monument, near Los Alamos, preserves cliff dwellings, a circular pueblo building that was originally three-stories high and contained some three hundred rooms, and other archaeological sites amid a 50-sq.-mi. (129-km²) wilderness area.

119

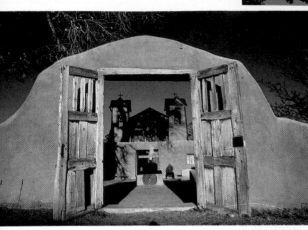

**Above: El Santuario de Chimayó
Right: San Felipe de Néri in the
Old Town section of Albuquerque**

Chaco Culture National Historical Park, near Farmington, preserves the ruins of a major center of the Anasazi culture. Pueblo Bonito, the largest of Chaco Canyon's brilliantly constructed pueblo ruins, was originally five-stories high, spread over 3 acres (1.2 hectares), and boasted more than eight hundred rooms.

El Morro National Monument, southwest of Grants, is the site of Inscription Rock, which bears the inscriptions of early Spanish explorers and westbound pioneers.

Fort Union National Monument, northeast of Las Vegas, preserves the ruins of an American fort that served from 1851 to 1891 as a key station along the long and dangerous Santa Fe Trail.

Gila Cliff Dwellings National Monument, north of Silver City, protects three groups of dwellings located in large caves cut into the canyon wall. These ancient "apartment buildings" were occupied by the Mogollon people from about A.D. 1 to 1300.

Old Town, the historic district of Albuquerque, features the town's original Plaza and the Church of San Felipe de Néri.

Pecos National Monument, southeast of Santa Fe, includes ruins of a fourteenth-century pueblo and a seventeenth-century Spanish mission.

Other Interesting Places to Visit:

Carlsbad Caverns National Park, near Carlsbad, features the world's most extensive and spectacular limestone caves. A series of about seventy underground chambers are strung along a 3-mi. (4.8-km) walk. The largest chamber, at a depth of more than 700 ft. (213 m), is as large as fourteen football fields and as tall as a twenty-two-story building.

City of Rocks State Park, northwest of Deming, is a cluster of interestingly shaped volcanic rock formations.

120

Mogollon, once a thriving mining center, is now one of New Mexico's many ghost towns.

El Santuario de Chimayó, in Chimayó, is sometimes called the Lourdes of America because of the healing powers attributed to mud taken from the chapel floor.

Ghost Towns, the abandoned remains of once-thriving frontier towns, may be found in almost every New Mexico county. One of the most interesting is *Mogollon* near Silver City, whose mines once produced millions of dollars' worth of gold and silver. Among New Mexico's many other ghost towns are *Colfax* and *Loma Parda* in the northeast part of the state; *White Oaks* in the southeast; *Elizabethtown* in north-central New Mexico; and *Chloride, Kelly, Lake Valley, Shakespeare, Steins,* and *Winston* in the southwest.

Four Corners Monument, near Farmington, marks the only spot in the United States where four states (New Mexico, Colorado, Arizona, and Utah) meet.

Gallup, called the "Indian Capital of the World," is the trading and marketing center for the Navajos, Zuñis, and Hopis, whose reservations are nearby. Its Inter-Tribal Indian Ceremonial, held annually since 1922, features traditional dress, rodeos, art fairs, and traditional songs and dances.

Pueblos, situated throughout the state, are the individual villages of New Mexico's nineteen Pueblo Indian groups. Visitors are welcome at all of the pueblos, but are requested to behave as would a guest in a private home. The best-known New Mexico pueblo is *Acoma*, situated about 50 mi. (80.4 km) west of Albuquerque. Established around A.D. 600, it is believed to be the oldest continuously occupied village in the United States. Also called "Sky City," Acoma is perched atop a huge, 365-foot- (111-meter-) high sandstone mesa. New Mexico's other pueblos, each of which gives visitors a fascinating glimpse of traditional arts and crafts, ceremonial dances, and a unique way of life, are: *Cochiti*, midway between Albuquerque and Santa Fe; *Isleta*, south of Albuquerque; *Jemez*, northwest of Bernalillo; *Laguna*, west of Albuquerque; *Nambe*, east of the town of Pojoaque; *Picuris*, south of Taos; *Pojoaque*, east of the town of Pojoaque; *San Felipe*, midway between Albuquerque and Santa Fe; *San Ildefonso*, east of Los Alamos; *San Juan*, north of Española; *Sandia*, north of Albuquerque; *Santa Ana*, west of Bernalillo; *Santa Clara*, south of Española; *Santo Domingo*, southwest of Santa Fe; *Taos*, near the town of Taos; *Tesuque*, north of Santa Fe; *Zia*, west of Bernalillo; and *Zuñi*, south of Gallup.

Sandia Peak Tram is the longest aerial tram in the United States.

Sandia Peak Tram, along Sandia Peak, is the nation's longest tramway, extending for 2.7 mi. (4.34 km). Riders on the tram travel up 4,000 ft. (1,219 m) in fifteen minutes to a spectacular view at the top.

Shiprock, south of the town of Shiprock, is an unusual rock formation that is said to resemble a ship in full sail.

Valle Grande, between Jemez Springs and Los Alamos, is the 176-sq.-mi. (456-km²) circular cone of an extinct volcano.

White Sands National Monument, near Alamogordo, is a 144,000-acre (58,277-hectare) desert of shimmering gypsum sand dunes. Nearby are the White Sands Missile Range; and Trinity Site, where the world's first atomic bomb was detonated.

IMPORTANT DATES

c. 500 B.C.-A.D. 1200—The Mogollon Culture thrives in what is now the southwestern part of the state

c. A.D. 1-1300—The Anasazi Culture rises and falls in northwestern New Mexico

600s—Pueblo of Acoma is established

1500s—Navajo, Apache, Ute, and Comanche groups enter New Mexico

1539—A group of Spaniards led by priest Marcos de Niza and a guide named Estevanico explore the New Mexico region

1540-1542—Francisco Vásquez de Coronado explores New Mexico and the Southwest in search of gold

1581—*El Camino Real* (the Royal Road), which runs from Santa Fe to the state of Chihuahua, Mexico and is the oldest road in the United States, is traveled for the first time by Augustín Rodríguez and Francisco Sánchez Chamuscado

1582—Antonio de Espejo explores the region along the Rio Grande; his report on the rich land and minerals there leads to the beginning of Spanish settlement in the territory

1598—Juan de Oñate establishes San Juan, the first permanent Spanish colony in what is now New Mexico

1610—Pedro de Peralta, Spanish governor of New Mexico, establishes a new capital at Santa Fe

1680—Popé leads the Pueblo people in a revolt against Spanish rule, forcing the Spaniards to retreat to Mexico

1692—Diego de Vargas enters Santa Fe and recaptures New Mexico for Spain

1706—Albuquerque is founded

1807—Zebulon Pike, exploring Spanish territories under the United States flag, is arrested by the Spaniards and brought to Santa Fe

1821—Mexico wins its independence from Spain and takes control of New Mexico; William Becknell opens the Santa Fe Trail by leading the first wagon train from Missouri to Santa Fe

1834—New Mexico's first newspaper, *El Crepúsculo de la Libertad* ("The Dawn of Liberty"), is established in Santa Fe

1837—Mexican and Indian citizens of New Mexico revolt against the Mexican colonial government, kill the Mexican governor, and install as governor a Taos Indian named José Gonzales; Mexican general Manuel Armijo leads a counterinsurgence, executes Gonzales, and succeeds him as governor

1841—General Hugh McLeod of the independent Republic of Texas invades New Mexico, but is defeated by Mexican troops

1846—The Mexican War breaks out; the United States takes possession of New Mexico after General Stephen Kearny captures Santa Fe without a fight

1847—The first English-language newspaper in New Mexico, the *Santa Fe Republican,* is published

1848—The Mexican War ends; Mexico cedes New Mexico to the United States

1849—Regular stagecoach service begins on the Santa Fe Trail

1850—The Territory of New Mexico is created by the United States Congress

1853—The Gadsden Purchase gives New Mexico its present southern border

A wagon train arriving at the Santa Fe Plaza in 1868

1858 — The Butterfield Trail, the first trail to run from California through southern New Mexico, is opened

1861 — New Mexico's northern boundary becomes fixed at the thirty-seventh parallel by the creation of the Territory of Colorado

1862 — Confederate troops occupy Albuquerque and Santa Fe; their defeat at Glorieta Pass keeps New Mexico a Union territory during the Civil War; General James Carleton arrives with a Union army to subdue the Navajos and Apaches

1863 — The creation of the Territory of Arizona gives New Mexico its present boundaries

1864 — Colonel Kit Carson defeats the Navajo; eight thousand Navajo are forced on the "Long Walk," a terrible, 300-mile (483-kilometer) march to the reservation at Bosque Redondo near Fort Sumner

1868 — The United States government allows the Navajos to return to their former homeland

1870 — Lucien Maxwell founds the First National Bank of Santa Fe

1875 — Roman Catholic bishop Jean Baptiste Lamy is named archbishop of Santa Fe

1878 — A range war known as the Lincoln County War is fought between rival cattlemen; Billy the Kid, an eventual folk hero, is a major participant in the gunfighting; the first railroad line in New Mexico Territory is laid across Raton Pass

1879 — Mescalero Apaches leave the Mescalero Reservation and wage frequent attacks against white settlers in New Mexico

1881 — Billy the Kid is killed by Sheriff Pat Garrett

1886 — Apache leader Geronimo is forced to surrender, ending Apache warfare against white settlers

1912 — New Mexico becomes the forty-seventh state

1916—Mexican revolutionary Pancho Villa and his men raid Columbus, setting houses on fire and killing sixteen citizens; General John Pershing is sent on a punitive expedition into Mexico

1922—New Mexico becomes an important oil-producing state with the discovery of Hogback and Rattlesnake oil fields in San Juan County and the Artesia oil field in Eddy County; novelist D.H. Lawrence arrives in Taos

1924—Congress passes the Pueblo Lands Act to evict squatters on Indian lands; Gila National Forest becomes the first officially designated United States Wilderness Area

1930—Carlsbad Caverns National Park is created

1931—Potash mining begins at Carlsbad, freeing the United States from dependency on the foreign potash monopoly

1943—The Manhattan Project, which resulted in the development of the first atomic bomb, begins secretly at Los Alamos

1945—The world's first atomic bomb is tested in the desert near Alamogordo

1948—As a result of a lawsuit, a court ruling recognizes voting rights for the Indians of New Mexico and Arizona

1949—Artist Georgia O'Keeffe settles in northern New Mexico

1950—Uranium ore is discovered in the northwest part of the state by Paddy Martinez, a Navajo prospector

1964—The San Juan-Chama water project, a plan to bring water to north-central New Mexico through a system of tunnels extending from the San Juan River, is started

1966—A new state capitol is completed

1967—Reies Tijerina and the Alianza Federal de Mercedes raid the Rio Arriba County Courthouse in Tierra Amarilla as part of a protest to restore community-owned land grants

1970—Congress recognizes the Taos Pueblo claim to possession of its sacred Blue Lake

1972—Harrison Schmitt of New Mexico becomes the first United States scientist-astronaut to land on the moon

1974—Robert Fortune Sanchez is ordained as archbishop of Santa Fe, becoming New Mexico's first Hispanic Roman Catholic bishop

1980—A prison riot at the New Mexico Penitentiary results in thirty-three deaths and $14 million in damage

1982—The United States Supreme Court rules that Indian nations or tribes may set a tax on the oil, natural gas, and minerals mined from Indian lands, upholding a 1976 tax levied by the Jicarilla Apaches

1986—Donald E. Pelotte is ordained bishop of Gallup, becoming the first Native-American Roman Catholic bishop

IMPORTANT PEOPLE

CLINTON ANDERSON

MARY AUSTIN

JUDY BLUME

Clinton Anderson (1895-1975), newspaperman and politician; settled in Albuquerque in 1917; U.S. representative (1941-45); U.S. secretary of agriculture (1945-48); U.S. senator (1949-75)

Mary Hunter Austin (1868-1934), author; settled in Santa Fe; best known for her first book, *The Land of Little Rain,* and for her play *The Arrow Maker,* both of which are sympathetic depictions of Indian life in the western United States

Elfego Baca (1865-1945), born in Socorro; lawyer and lawman; became a Mexican-American folk hero after an 1882 shootout in which he, as deputy sheriff, jailed a Texas cowboy and held him prisoner for thirty-six hours while eighty angry and armed cowboys tried to free their friend

Adolph Francis Alphonse Bandelier (1840-1914), historian and archaeologist; lived among the Pueblo Indians (1880-86) while studying their life and culture; among his works about Indians are *Final Report on Indians of the Southwestern United States* and a novel, *The Delight Makers;* Bandelier National Monument is named in his honor

William Becknell (1796?-1865), explorer and trader; known as the "Father of the Santa Fe Trail"; traveled from Missouri to Santa Fe in 1821 and again in 1822, establishing the route that became known as the Santa Fe Trail

Charles Bent (1799-1847), fur trader and territorial governor; builder of Bent's Fort, a landmark of the Santa Fe Trail; later settled at Taos; served as first civil governor after the U.S. took possession of New Mexico (1846-47); assassinated by a group of Hispanics and Indians who were rebelling against American rule

Judy Blume (1938-   ), writer; resides in Santa Fe; specializes in novels that deal frankly with adolescents' problems; her best-known works include *Are You There God? It's Me, Margaret* and the adult books *Wifey* and *Smart Women*

Ernest Leonard Blumenschein (1874-1960), artist; best known for his paintings of Taos Indians; founded the famous Taos art colony with fellow artist Bert Phillips

William H. "Billy the Kid" Bonney, born Henry McCarty (1859?-1881); legendary outlaw and cattle rustler in New Mexico Territory; gunfighter in the Lincoln County War between cattle barons in the 1870s; murdered at least twenty-one people before being killed by Lincoln County sheriff Pat Garrett

James H. Carleton (1814-1873), career army officer; active in American campaigns against the Navajos and the Apaches in the 1860s

JAMES CARLETON

Christopher (Kit) Carson (1809-1868), frontiersman, guide, explorer, Indian agent, and Indian fighter; trapper (1831-42); settled in Taos; appointed Indian Agent to the Utes (1853-61); commanded the 1st New Mexico Volunteers during the Civil War; supervised the "Long Walk" (1864) in which thousands of captured Indians were marched forcibly across New Mexico for resettlement at Bosque Redondo; was later active in having the Navajos returned to their homeland

Willa Sibert Cather (1873-1947), author and editor; Santa Fe resident noted for her novels of pioneer life; received the 1923 Pulitzer Prize in fiction for *One of Ours*; her novel *Death Comes for the Archbishop* describes the life of Jean Baptiste Lamy

Thomas Benton Catron (1840-1921), lawyer and politician; became one of New Mexico's first U.S. senators (1913)

KIT CARSON

Dionisio (Dennis) Chavez (1888-1962), born in Los Chavez; politician; U.S. representative (1931-35); U.S. senator (1935-62); influential and able spokesman in Washington for Indians, Hispanics, and other minority groups; helped establish the federal Fair Employment Practices Commission

John Simpson Chisum (1824-1884), cattleman, frontiersman; pioneered cattle-ranching and trail-herding in New Mexico; at its height, his New Mexico ranch spread over 200 miles (322 kilometers) and boasted the largest cattle herd in the world; Indian raids, rustlers, competition, and his involvement in the Lincoln County War combined to reduce his power and wealth

WILLA CATHER

Cochise (1812?-1874), chief of the Chiricahua Apaches in southeastern Arizona; lived at peace with white settlers until 1861, when he was falsely accused of kidnapping and was captured by federal authorities; though he escaped, his fellow Apache prisoners were hung; in an attempt to regain Indian lands that had been taken by ranchers and U.S. bureaucrats, led his warriors on raids against southwestern ranches, stagecoaches, and mining sites; was forced to surrender in 1871

Francisco Vásquez de Coronado (1510?-1554), Spanish explorer; searched New Mexico (1540-42) for the legendary Seven Golden Cities of Cíbola but found only the Zuñi pueblos; his account of his trip was the first European description of what is now the southwestern United States

DENNIS CHAVEZ

ALBERT FALL

GERONIMO

LAURA GILPIN

ROBERT GODDARD

Frank Hamilton Cushing (1857-1900), pioneer ethnologist of the Southwest; studied the culture, language and folklore of ancient and contemporary Indians; lived with the Zuñi for five years and was adopted by them

Estevanico, also known as Estévan or Estéban (1500?-1539), North African explorer; one of the first explorers of the Southwest; his false tales of gold inspired expeditions into New Mexico by Father Marcos de Niza and Francisco Vásquez de Coronado; killed by Zuñi Indians while acting as guide for de Niza

Albert Bacon Fall (1861-1944), lawyer, rancher, miner, and public official; U.S. senator from New Mexico (1912-21); U.S. secretary of the interior (1921-23); in 1929 was convicted of bribery and conspiracy for granting leases without competitive bidding in what became known as the Teapot Dome Scandal

Erna Fergusson (1888-1964), born in Albuquerque; author and local historian; portrayed life in New Mexico; her *Dancing Gods* describes Indian ceremonials

Harvey Fergusson (1890-1971), born in Albuquerque; author; known for realistic novels of New Mexico life, especially his trilogy about the Santa Fe Trail: *Blood of the Conquerors, Wolf Song,* and *In Those Days*

Patrick Floyd (Pat) Garrett (1850-1908), buffalo hunter, cowboy, horse rancher, Texas Ranger, and lawman; became famous as the New Mexico sheriff who hunted down and finally shot Billy the Kid

Geronimo (1829-1909), leader of the Chiricahua Apaches; his family was murdered by the Mexicans; was widely feared for his fierce surprise attacks in both the New Mexico Territory and in Mexico; although he was captured several times and sent to a reservation, he escaped to raid again until he finally surrendered in 1886

Laura Gilpin (1891-1979), photographer; specialized in photographing the people of the Navajo and Pueblo cultures and the landscape of New Mexico and the Southwest

Robert Hutchings Goddard (1882-1945), physicist; pioneered modern rocket and space technology; tested first successful liquid-fueled rocket; was granted more than two hundred rocketry patents; did much of his later research in Roswell; the National Aeronautics and Space Administration named its Goddard Space Flight Center in his honor

R.C. Gorman (1932-   ), internationally known Navajo artist; best known for his paintings of Navajo women; resides in Taos, where he owns an art gallery

Carl Atwood Hatch (1889-1963), jurist, politician; New Mexico state district judge (1923-29), U.S. senator (1933-49); U.S. district judge for New Mexico (1949-62); best known for the Hatch Act of 1939, which limits the political activities of federal employees

Conrad Nicholson Hilton (1887-1979), born in San Antonio; hotel entrepreneur; New Mexico state representative (1912-13); in 1919, bought his first hotel in Texas and built it up into the Hilton International Corporation, the world's largest hotel chain

Paul Horgan (1903-   ), author and local historian; grew up in New Mexico; often uses the state as the subject of his novels and historical writing; received the Pulitzer Prize in history in 1955 for *Great River: The Rio Grande in North American History*, and in 1976 for *Lamy of Santa Fe*

PAUL HORGAN

Peter Hurd (1904-1984), born in Roswell; artist; noted for his realistic paintings of southwestern scenes and for his portraits

Stephen Watts Kearny (1794-1848), army officer; as commander of the United States Army of the West during the Mexican War, he led the forces that occupied New Mexico and California

Oliver Hazard Perry La Farge (1901-1963), anthropologist and author; best known for his novel *Laughing Boy*, which received the 1930 Pulitzer Prize in fiction, and for such works dealing with Indian culture as *All the Young Men* and *The Enemy Gods*

PETER HURD

Jean Baptiste Lamy (1814-1888), French-American missionary; first resident Roman Catholic bishop in New Mexico; bishop of Santa Fe (1851); archbishop of Santa Fe (1875-85); established schools, missions, hospitals, and a cathedral in Santa Fe; his life became the basis for Willa Cather's novel *Death Comes for the Archbishop*

David Herbert (D.H.) Lawrence (1885-1930), English novelist, poet, and social critic; settled in Taos and is buried there; best known for frank depictions of relationships between men and women in such novels as *Lady Chatterley's Lover*, *Women in Love*, and *Sons and Lovers*; his poems in *Birds, Beasts and Flowers* reflect the beauty he found in New Mexico

STEPHEN W. KEARNY

Mabel Dodge Luhan (1879-1962), writer; settled in Taos and married Taos Indian Tony Luhan; influenced other writers and artists to move to the community with such books as *Lorenzo in Taos*, about English author D.H. Lawrence, and *Taos and its Artists*

Manuelito (1818-1893), Navajo leader; fought to prevent white settlers from taking over Indian lands in the Southwest; in 1860, led attack on Fort Defiance in Arizona; resisted capture by the U.S. cavalry; surrendered only to save family and followers from starvation; was instrumental in securing permission for the Navajo to return to their homeland after their imprisonment at Bosque Redondo

José Antonio Martinez (1793-1867), born in Abiquiu; Taos Roman Catholic priest; worked to bring education and justice to poor Hispanics and Indians; his political and antiestablishment activities led to excommunication by Bishop Lamy in 1854

MABEL DODGE LUHAN

BILL MAULDIN

JOSEPH MONTOYA

GEORGIA O'KEEFFE

ROBERT OPPENHEIMER

Maria Antonita Martinez (1887-1980), potter; led an artistic revival of the ancient art of Pueblo pottery-making; noted for her interpretation and execution of the traditional "black-on-black" pottery of San Ildefonso Pueblo

William Henry (Bill) Mauldin (1921-   ), born in Mountain Park; cartoonist; famous for his World War II cartoons for the U.S. armed forces newspaper *Stars and Stripes*; Pulitzer Prizewinning editorial cartoonist for the *St. Louis Post-Dispatch* and the *Chicago Sun-Times*; his war cartoons are collected in *Up Front*

Mark Howard Medoff (1940-   ), playwright; in 1966 became a professor of drama at New Mexico State University at Las Cruces; in 1975 was named Dramatist-in-Residence at the university; best known for his award-winning play *Children of a Lesser God*, which was made into a movie in 1986

Joseph M. Montoya (1915-1978), born in Peña Blanca; politician; New Mexico state representative (1937-40); state senator (1940-46); lieutenant governor (1947-51, 1955-57); U.S. senator (1965-77)

John Nichols (1940-   ), author; noted for such realistic novels of contemporary New Mexico life as *The Milagro Beanfield War*

Georgia O'Keeffe (1887-1986), painter; in 1929 spent a summer in New Mexico; the stark beauty of the desert landscape so appealed to her that she settled there permanently in 1949; her subjects were usually objects in nature, such as rocks, flowers, clouds, and animal bones, that have been reduced to their simplest forms and colors

Juan de Oñate (1550?-1630), Spanish explorer; colonizer of New Mexico; first Spanish royal governor of New Mexico (1595-1607); founded San Juan in 1598

Robert Oppenheimer (1904-1967), physicist; directed the Manhattan Project at Los Alamos, which developed the world's first atomic bomb (1942-45); chair of the General Advisory Committee of the Atomic Energy Commission (1947-53); received the Enrico Fermi Award (1963)

John Joseph "Black Jack" Pershing (1860-1948), career army officer; served in the 1886 Apache Indian campaign in New Mexico and Arizona; commanded the 1916 penetration of U.S. forces into Chihuahua to punish Mexico's revolutionary leader Pancho Villa for raids in New Mexico; best known as commander of the American Expeditionary Forces (AEF) in World War I

Bert Greer Phillips (1868-1956), artist; co-founder of the Taos art colony; specialized in painting Indian subjects

Zebulon Montgomery Pike (1779-1813), career army officer, explorer; his *Journal of a Tour Through the Interior Parts of New Spain,* which described his experiences in Santa Fe and the Southwest, stimulated westward American expansion

Popé (1630?-1692), San Juan Pueblo leader; led the Pueblo Revolt (1680), in which the Pueblo people rebelled against Spanish oppression; after succeeding in driving the Spaniards out of New Mexico, worked to erase the influences of Spanish culture while reestablishing traditional Pueblo religion and culture

Edmund Gibson Ross (1885-1889), public official; governor of New Mexico Territory (1885-89); signed the bill that created a university at Albuquerque, an agricultural college at Las Cruces, and a mining school at Socorro

EDMUND ROSS

Harrison Hagan Schmitt (1935-   ), born in Santa Rita; geologist, politician; participated in the 1972 Apollo 17 mission as the first American scientist-astronaut to make a space flight; during his seventy-five-hour visit to the moon (the longest ever), he studied the lunar surface and took rock samples for future analysis; U.S. senator (1977-83)

Joseph Henry Sharp (1859-1953), artist; early member of the Taos art community; noted for his portraits of famous Indians of his day

HARRISON SCHMITT

John Sloan (1871-1951), artist; member of the "Ashcan School," a group of American artists who portrayed realistic scenes of urban life; became a member of the Santa Fe art community in the early 1920s; painted realistic scenes of Indian life; best known for promoting public awareness of such modern art movements as Cubism and Expressionism

Reies Lopez Tijerina (1926-   ), political activist; founder and president of the Alianza Federal de Mercedes, a militant Hispanic group seeking the return of Mexican land grants; in 1967, he and the group took over the county courthouse in Tierra Amarilla; during the raid, hostages were taken and two officers were shot; was acquitted after being arrested and tried for the incident; was subsequently convicted of and jailed on various federal charges

JOHN SLOAN

Al Unser (1939-   ), born in Albuquerque; race-car driver; four-time winner of the Indianapolis 500; two-time winner of the Pike's Peak Hill Climb; in 1970 placed first in the United States Auto Club (USAC) National Championship rankings; has won thirty-five National Championship races during his career

Robert William (Bobby) Unser (1934-   ), born in Albuquerque; race-car driver; three-time winner of the Indianapolis 500; twelve-time winner of the Pike's Peak Hill Climb; placed first in the United States Auto Club (USAC) National Championship rankings in 1968 and 1974; has won more than twenty-five National Championship races

Diego de Vargas (1643-1704), Spanish soldier and administrator; reconquered New Mexico for Spain in 1692 after the 1680 Pueblo Revolt; became governor of the reclaimed territory (1691-97, 1703-04)

DIEGO DE VARGAS

LEW WALLACE

Victorio (1825?-1881), chief and military leader of the Mimbreno Apaches; military genius who thwarted the armies of the United States and Mexico for fifteen months, from 1879 until his death, while his raiding warriors terrorized New Mexico, Arizona, and Mexico in a vain effort to reclaim their traditional lands in the Black Mountains

Lewis (Lew) Wallace (1827-1905), soldier, politician, author; territorial governor of New Mexico (1878-81); best known for his popular novel *Ben-Hur*

GOVERNORS

William C. McDonald	1912-1917
Ezequiel Caba de Baca	1917
Washington E. Lindsey	1917-1919
Octaviano A. Larrazolo	1919-1921
Merritt C. Mechem	1921-1923
James F. Hinkle	1923-1925
Arthur T. Hannett	1925-1927
Richard C. Dillon	1927-1931
Arthur Seligman	1931-1933
A. W. Hockenhull	1933-1935
Clyde Tingley	1935-1939
John E. Miles	1939-1943
John L. Dempsey	1943-1947
Thomas L. Mabry	1947-1951
Edwin L. Mechem	1951-1955
John F. Simms	1955-1957
Edwin L. Mechem	1957-1959
John Burroughs	1959-1961
Edwin L. Mechem	1961-1962
Tom Bolack (acting)	1962-1963
Jack M. Campbell	1963-1967
David F. Cargo	1967-1971
Bruce King	1971-1975
Jerry Apodaca	1975-1979
Bruce King	1979-1983
Toney Anaya	1983-1987
Garrey E. Carruthers	1987-

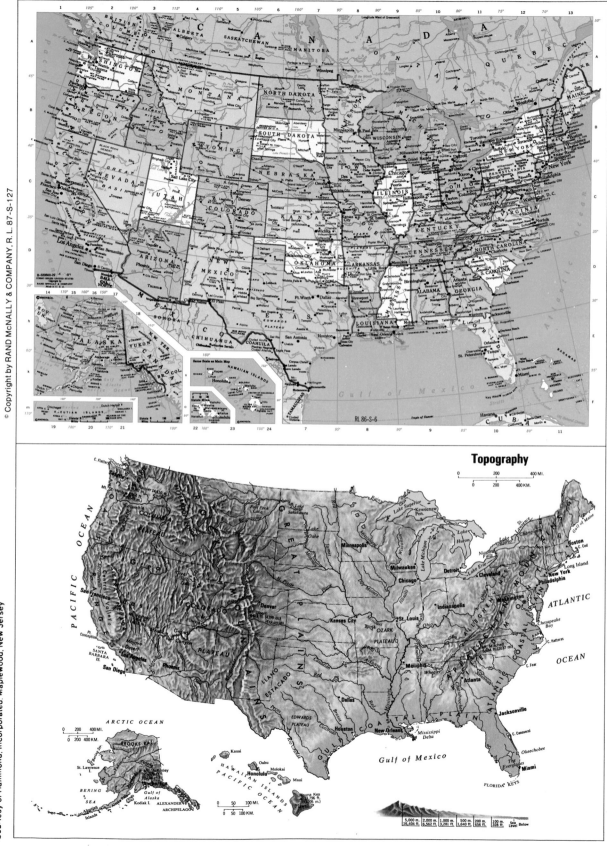

Topography

MAP KEY

Name	Grid	Name	Grid
Abiquiu	A5	Contreras	B5
Abo	B5	Corona	B6
Acoma Indian Reservation	B5	Costilla	A6
Air Base City	C7	Coyote	A5
Alameda	B5;E6	Crossroads	C7
Alamogordo	C6	Crownpoint	B4
Alamogordo Reservoir (reservoir)	B6	Crystal	A4
Albert	B7	Cuba	B5
Albuquerque	B5;E6	Cubero	B5
Alcalde	A5	Cuchillo	C5
Algodones	B5;E6	Cuervo	B6
Allimaso Creek (creek)	B6,7	Datil	B5
Amalia	A6	Deming	C5
Amistad	B7	Des Moines	A7
Ancho	C6	Dexter	C6
Animas	D4	Dilia	B6;E7
Anton Chico	B6;E7	Dixon	A6
Apache Creek	C4	Doña Ana	C5
Arabela	C6	Dora	C7
Aragon	C4	Dulce	A5
Arch	B7	Dunlap	B6
Armijo	E6	Duran	B6
Arrey	C5	Eagle Nest	A6
Arroyo Hondo	A6	El Pueblo	E7
Arroyo Seco	A6	El Rito	A5
Artesia	C6	Elephant Butte Reservoir (reservoir)	C5
Aztec	A5	Elida	C7
Azul	D7	Elk	C6
Bayard	C4	Elkins	C6
Belen	B5	Encino	B6
Bennett	C7	Engle	C5
Bent	C6	Ensenada	A5
Berino	C5	Escobas Peak (peak)	D7
Bernalillo	B5;E6	Española	B5
Bibo	B5	Estancia	B5
Biklabito	A4	Eunice	C7
Blanchard	E7	Fairacres	C5
Blanco	A5	Farley	A6
Bloomfield	A5	Farmington	A4
Bluewater	B5	Fence Lake	B4
Boles	C5	Flora Vista	A4
Bosque	B5	Floyd	B7
Brazos Peak (peak)	A5	Flying H	C6
Broadview	B7	Folsom	A7
Buckeye	C7	Forrest	B7
Buckhorn	C4	Fort Bayard	C4
Buena Vista	B6	Fort Stanton	C6
Bueyeros	B7	Fort Sumner	B6
Canadian River (river)	A6;B6,7	Fort Wingate	B4
Canjilon	A5	Gabaldon	D7
Canyon	D6	Gage	C4
Canyoncito	D7	Galisteo	B6;E7
Capitan	C6	Gallup	B4
Caprock	C7	Gamerco	B4
Capulin	A7	Garfield	C5
Carlsbad	C6	Gila	C4
Carrizozo	C6	Gila River (river)	C4
Causey	C7	Gladstone	A7
Cebolla	A5	Glencoe	C6
Cedar Crest	E6	Glenrio	B7
Cedar Hill	A5	Glenwood	C4
Cedarvale	B6	Glorieta	B6;D7
Central	C4	Grady	B7
Cerrillos	B5;E6	Grants	B5
Chaco River (river)	A,B4	Grenville	A7
Chacon	A5	Guadalupita	A6
Chama	A5	Hachita	C4
Chamberino	C5	Hagerman	C6
Chapelle	B6;E7	Hanover	C4
Chilili	B5	Happy Valley	C6
Chimayo	B6	Hatch	C5
Cimarron	A6	Hayden	B7
Claunch	B5,6	Helweg	E6
Clayton	A7	Heron Reservoir (reservoir)	A5
Cleveland	A6	Hillsboro	C5
Cliff	C4	Hobbs	C7
Cloudcroft	C6	Hollywood	C6
Clovis	B7	Hondo	C6
Cochiti	D6	Hope	C6
Colmor	A6	Horse Springs	C4
Columbus	D5	House	B6
Conchas Dam	B6	Humble City	C7
Conchas Reservoir (reservoir)	B6	Hurley	C4
Continental Divide (divide) A5;B5,4;C4,5,4;D4		Ilfeld	E7

Name	Grid	Name	Grid
Isleta	B5	Placitas	B5;E6
Isleta Indian Reservation	B5	Pleasant Hill	B7
Jal	C7	Polvadera	B5
Jarales	B5	Ponderosa	B5
Jemez Canyon Flood Control Reservoir (flood control reservoir)	B5	Portales	B7
Jemez Pueblo	B5;D6	Puerco River (river)	B4,5
Jemez River (river)	D,E6	Puerto de Luna	B6
Jemez Springs	B5	Quemado	B4
Jicarilla Indian Reservation	A5	Questa	A6
Kelly	B5	Ramah	B4
Kingston	C5	Ranches of Taos	A6
Kinney	E6	Raton	A6
Lake McMillan (lake)	D6	Red Hill	B4
La Bajada	B6	Bedrock	C4
La Cueva	A5	Rehoboth	B4
La Jara	C6	Rencona	B6;E7
La Luz	C6	Reserve	C4
La Madera	A5	Ribera	E7
La Mesa	C5	Rincon	C5
Laguna	B5	Rio Chama (river)	A5
Laguna Indian Reservation	B5	Rio Grande (river)	A6,5;B,C,D5/D,E6
Lajoya	B5	Rio Puerco (river)	A,B5
Lake Arthur	C6	Rociada	B6
Lakewood	C6	Rocky Mountains (mountains)	A,B,C6
Lamy	A6	Rodeo	D4
Las Cruces	C5	Rogers	C7
Las Palama	C6	Romero	D7
Las Tablas	A5	Roswell	C6
Las Vegas	B6;D7	Rowe	E7
Ledoux	B6	Roy	B6
Lemitar	B5	Ruidoso	C6
Leyba	B6;E7	Ruidoso Downs	C6
Line Mountain (mountain)	C4	Sabinoso	B6
Lincoln	C6	Salem	B5
Lindrith	A5	San Acacia	B5
Lingo	C7	San Antonio	C5
Llano	A6	San Felipe	B5
Llano Estacado (plain)	B,C7	San Fidel	B5
Loco Hills	C7	San Francisco River (river)	C4
Logan	B7	San Jon	B7
Lordsburg	C4	San Jose	B6;E7
Los Alamos	B5	San Juan	A4
Los Lunas	B5	San Juan River (river)	A4,5
Los Pinos	A5	San Mateo	B5
Los Vigiles	D7	San Miguel	C5;E7
Loving	C6	San Patricio	C6
Lovington	C7	San Rafael	B5
Lumberton	A5	San Ysidro	D6
Luna	C4	Sandoval	B5;E6
Madrid	B5;E6	Santa Fe	B6;D7
Maes	B6	Santa Rita	C4
Magdalena	B5	Santa Rosa	B6
Malaga	C6	Santo Domingo Pueblo	B5;D6
Maljamar	C7	Scholle	B5
Manzano	B5	Seama	B5
Marquez	B5	Seboyeta	B5
Maxwell	A6	Sedan	A7
Mayhill	C6	Sena	B6;E7
McDonald	C7	Sepan	C4
McIntosh	B5	Serafina	E7
Melrose	B7	Shiprock	A4
Mentmore	B4	Silver City	C4
Mesa Chivato (mesa)	B5	Socorro	B5
Mescalero	C6	Soham	E7
Mescalero Apache Indian Reservation	C6	Solano	B6
Mesilla	C5	Springer	A6
Mesilla Park	C5	St. vrain	B7
Mesquite	C5	Stanley	B5,6;E6,7
Mexican Springs	B4	Sunland Park	D5
Miami	A6	Sunspot	C6
Mills	A6	Taiban	B6
Mogollon	C4	Tajique	B5
Monero	A5	Taos	A6
Montezuma	B6;D7	Tapia	E7
Monticello	C5	Tatum	C7
Montoya	B6	Tecolote	E7
Monument	C7	Texico	B7
Mora	B6	Thoreau	B4
Moriarty	B5	Three Rivers	C5
Mosquero	B7	Tierra Amarilla	A5
Mountainair	B5	Tijeras	E6
Mount Dora	A7	Toadlena	A4
Nara Visa	B7	Tocito	A4
Navajo Indian Reservation	A,B4	Tohatchi	B4
Navajo Reservoir (reservoir)	A5	Tolar	B7
New Laguna	B5	Tome	B5
Newcomb	A4	Torreon	B5
Newkirk	B6	Trementina	B6
Norton	B7	Truchas	A6
Oil Center	C7	Trujillo	B6
Ojo Caliente	A5	Truth or Consequences	C5
Ojo Feliz	A6	Tucumcari	B7
Orchard Park	C6	Tularosa	C5
Organ	C5	Tyrone	C4
Orogrande	C5	University Park	C5
Oscuro	C5	Ute Mountain Indian Reservation	A4
Oscura Peak (peak)	C5	Vado	C5
Otis	C6	Valle Grande Mountains (mountains)	D6
Padilla Creek (creek)	B,C6	Vallecitos	A5
Paguate	B5	Valley Ranch	D7
Pastura	B6	Vallecitos	A5
Pecos	D7	Veguita	B5
Pecos River (river)	A,B,C6;D,E7	Velarde	A5,6
Pedernal Peak (peak)	B6	Villanueva	B6;E7
Penablanca	B5;D6	Virden	C4
Penasco	A6	Wagon Mound	A6
Pep	C7	Waldo	E6
Peralta	B5	Waterflow	A4
Petaca	A5,6	Watrous	B6
Picacho	C6	Weed	C6
Pie Town	B4	Wheeler Peak (peak)	A6
Pine	B6;D7	Whites City	C6
Pinon	C6	Willard	B5
Pinos Altos	C4	Winston	C5
		Yeso	B6
		Zuñi Indian Reservation	B4

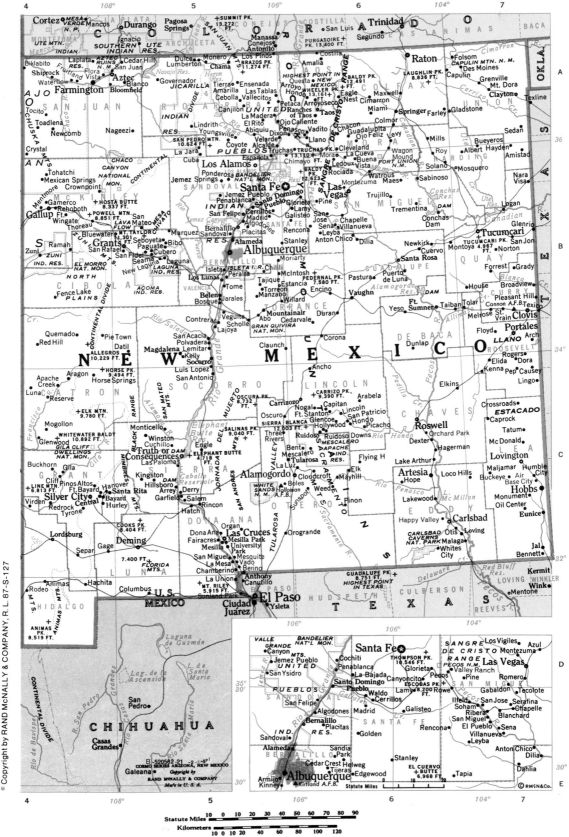

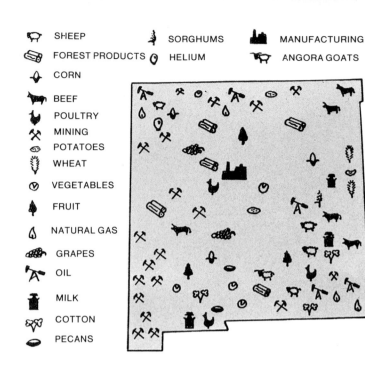

- 🐑 SHEEP
- 🪵 FOREST PRODUCTS
- CORN
- BEEF
- POULTRY
- ⛏️ MINING
- POTATOES
- WHEAT
- VEGETABLES
- FRUIT
- NATURAL GAS
- GRAPES
- OIL
- MILK
- COTTON
- PECANS

- 🐖 SORGHUMS
- HELIUM
- 🏭 MANUFACTURING
- ANGORA GOATS

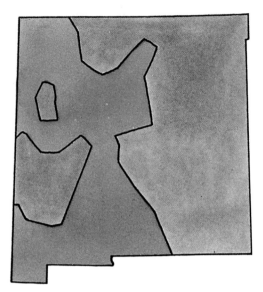

AVERAGE YEARLY PRECIPITATION

Centimeters		Inches
30 to 61		12 to 24
0 to 30		0 to 12

POPULATION DENSITY

Number of persons per square kilometer		Number of persons per square mile
More than 10		More than 25
4 to 10		10 to 25
2 to 4		5 to 10
Less than 2		Less than 5

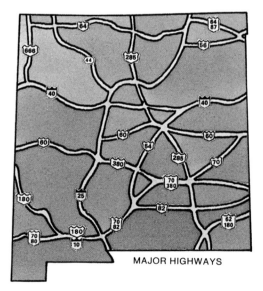

MAJOR HIGHWAYS

TOPOGRAPHY

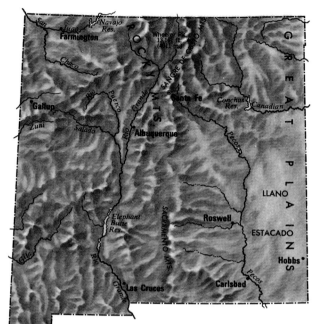

| Below Sea Level | 100 m. 328 ft. | 200 m. 656 ft. | 500 m. 1,640 ft. | 1,000 m. 3,281 ft. | 2,000 m. 6,562 ft. | 5,000 m. 16,404 ft. |

Courtesy of Hammond, Incorporated
Maplewood, New Jersey

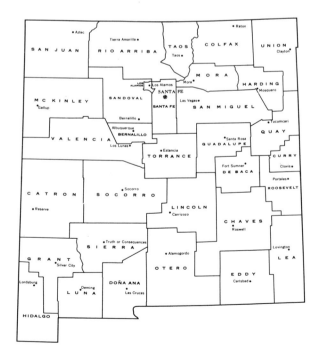

COUNTIES

The Rio Grande at Sandia Crest in central New Mexico

INDEX

Page numbers that appear in boldface type indicate illustrations.

The Cumbres & Toltec Scenic Railway zig-zags through north-central New Mexico from Chama to Antonita, Colorado.

Laguna Pueblo

Picture Identifications
Front cover: Fasada Butte at Chaco Culture National Historical Park
Back cover: Taos Pueblo
Pages 2-3: Dusk in Hernandez
Page 6: Luminarias in Old Town, Albuquerque
Pages 8-9: Shiprock
Pages 18-19: Montage of New Mexico residents that includes (page 18, clockwise from top left) a Navajo apple picker, a Navajo flagperson, a Zuñi woman performing the Butterfly Dance at Zuñi Pueblo, a Hispanic boy holding a chile pepper, an Acoma woman selling fresh-baked goods, and two Anglo farm boys; and (page 19, clockwise from top left), an Anglo farmer, a performer in the Comanche Dance at San Juan Pueblo, a Hispanic woman in the restored Spanish colonial town of Las Golindrinas, children playing at Kit Carson Park in Taos, a fisherman in the Pecos Wilderness, and drummers at Santa Clara Pueblo
Page 28: Anasazi ruins at Chaco Canyon National Historical Park
Page 36: San Miguel Mission in Santa Fe, the oldest church in the United States
Page 48: A wagon train along the Santa Fe Trail
Page 62: A rocket displayed at the International Space Hall of Fame in Alamogordo
Page 72: The Very Large Array near Socorro, the most powerful radio telescope in the world
Pages 80-81: The International Balloon Fiesta in Albuquerque
Pages 94-95: Horses grazing in northwestern New Mexico
Page 108: Montage showing the state flag, the state tree (piñon), the state gem (turquoise), the state bird (roadrunner), the state flower (yucca flower), and the state animal (black bear)

Picture Acknowledgments

Root Resources: © Byron Crader: Front cover, Page 35 (left); © Stephen Trimble: Pages 2-3, 8-9, 11 (top), 13 (bottom left), 18 (top right), 19 (top right, middle left), 24 (right), 26, 33 (top left), 85 (middle right), 142; © James Blank: Pages 4, 36, 80-81, 100 (right); © Kent & Donna Danner: Pages 43 (right), 97; © Ray Hillstrom: Page 58 (bottom left); © John Apolinski: Page 108 (turquoise); © Kenneth W. Fink: Page 108 (piñon)

H. Armstrong Roberts, Inc.: © R. Krubner: Page 5; © David Muench: Page 138

Journalism Services: © Ron Behrmann: Pages 6, 28, 30, 62, 87 (bottom right), 91, 93, 105 (left), 108 (yucca), 120 (right), 121, 122; © Dave Brown: Page 13 (top right); © Rich Clark: Page 108 (roadrunner)

© **Buddy Mays:** Pages 11 (bottom), 15 (both photos), 16, 18 (top left, middle left, bottom right), 19 (top left, bottom right, bottom left), 22, 23 (both photos), 33 (top right, bottom right), 45, 71, 76 (right), 78 (right), 86, 90, 105 (right), 106, 108 (bear), 120 (left), 128 (Gilpin)

Marilyn Gartman Agency: © Christy Volpe: Page 13 (top left, bottom right)

© **Reinhard Brucker:** Pages 13 (center), 33 (bottom left), 35 (right), 42, 74, 75, 85 (top left, top right, bottom right), 87 (top right)

Odyssey Productions: © Walter Frerck: Pages 14, 17 (left); © Robert Frerck: Pages 18 (middle right), 21, 24 (left), 41, 76 (left), 87 (top left), 94-95, 101 (left), Back cover

EKM Nepenthe: © Gildemeister: Page 17 (right); © R.V. Eckert, Jr.: Pages 19 (middle), 32, 72, 78 (left), 79, 87 (middle right), 103, 116; © Ted Rice: Page 43 (left)

© **Bob Skelly:** Pages 18 (bottom left), 69, 77 (left)

Historical Pictures Service, Inc., Chicago: Pages 39, 48, 50 (both photos), 51, 55 (right), 84 (right), 124, 126 (Anderson, Austin), 127 (Chavez), 128 (Geronimo), 129 (Kearny), 130 (Montoya), 131 (Ross), 132

© **Virginia Grimes:** Page 40

© **Lee Foster:** Pages 55 (left), 101 (right), 119

Museum of New Mexico: Pages 56, 58 (top left, right), 59, 60, 61, 64, 84 (left), 127 (Carleton, Carson), 131 (Vargas)

New Mexico State Records Center and Archives: Page 65

Wide World: Pages 67 (both photos), 83, 126 (Blume), 127 (Cather), 128 (Fall, Goddard), 129 (Horgan, Hurd, Luhan), 130 (O'Keeffe), 131 (Schmitt, Sloan)

© **Karen Yops:** Pages 77 (right), 85 (bottom left), 87 (bottom left)

© **Jerry Hennen:** Pages 98, 141

Cameramann International Ltd.: Page 100 (left)

Nawrocki Stock Photo: Page 113

UPI/Bettmann: Page 130 (Mauldin, Oppenheimer)

Courtesy Flag Research Center, Winchester, Massachusetts 01890: Flag on page 108

Len W. Meents: Maps on pages 97, 98, 101, 103, 105, 106, 136

About the Author

R. Conrad Stein was born and grew up in Chicago. He received a degree in history from the University of Illinois, and later studied at the University of Guanajuato in Mexico. Mr. Stein is the author of many books for young readers. He now lives in Chicago with his wife and their daughter Janna.

Before their daughter was born, the author and his wife lived for a brief period in Santa Fe, New Mexico. They loved the city, traveled extensively in the state, and agree that New Mexico is truly the Land of Enchantment.